# EVERY PARENT CAN

# Teach

## THEIR

# Toddler

---

## LEARNING THROUGH PLAY EVERY DAY

EDITED & PUBLISHED BY KARA CARRERO
ALLTERNATIVELEARNING.COM

Every Parent Can Teach their Toddler:
Learning through Play Every Day

Copyright © 2014-2015
Kara Carrero, Erin Buhr, Katie T. Christiansen, Jennifer Tammy
Monica Pruett, Becky Marie, Amanda Boyarshinov, Emma Edwards,
Monique B., Danielle Shaber, Birute Efe, Melissa Misra, Kimberly
Huff, Heather Greutman, Ashley Fratello, Kim Vij, Viviana Florea,
Alecia Francois, Vanessa Thiel, and Lindsay Eidhal.

ISBN-10: 1503091783
ISBN-13: 978-1503091788

Thank you for respecting the hard work of the editor and all of the contributors.

# Table of Contents

Because the toddler years are full of wonder and excitement, it's the perfect time to engage children in meaningful play and embrace their eagerness to learn.

This book is full of ideas and experiences from real life parents that have chosen to tot-school. Whether you choose just a few minutes a day or follow more of a routine, there are activities and resources to help find what works for your own family!

- Kara Carrero, editor, & writer at ALLterNATIVElearning.com

**USING THE BOOK**

If you're wanting to teach your toddler, but don't know where to start or you are already working with your child, there are activities and topics to cover everyone's needs.

## AUTHORS

All contributors are very talented bloggers who are passionate about kids and learning. Please visit their websites to find out more about them and what they do and follow them on social media to connect!

## LINKS WITHIN THE BOOK

You'll notice that throughout the book there are links to contributors' blogs and QR codes for accessibility to contributors' sites.

These links make this book a living and morphing project because of the new content on each writer's site. Our contributors would love for you visit their other resources and become part of their community.

## SUPERVISION & AGE APPROPRIATENESS

Activities and resources provided are based upon the experiences of the blogger who wrote them and the age and development level of their children

This means that only you can know what is appropriate for your child. If you do not feel comfortable completing an idea with your child, save it for a later date!

## A NOTE ABOUT TOT-SCHOOL

You will see this term used in different forms throughout the book. All similar terms refer to teaching a child that is approximately 10-36 months old.

The term "tot school" was trademarked and originally used by Carisa Hinson of 1+1+1=1. While she is not a contributing author, we would like to give her credit for the term.

# *What is Tot-School?*
## BY KARA CARRERO OF
## ALLTERNATIVELEARNING

## What is Tot-Schooling?

Tot-schooling is the means of raising a curious and hungry-to-learn child. It is exposing our toddlers to the world around them including diversity, multiculturalism, bilingualism, and simply every day practical life. It does not take a lot of money, time, or energy; it simply is about educating even the smallest children through play and exploration. It is part of parenting with a purpose, and it's the most rewarding part of my personal day.

Both pre-school and tot-school are so much more than learning facts and are so much more important than memorization. It is about raising life-long learners that appreciate the value of reading, exploring, learning, and playing!

## Why Tot-School?

As parents, it is our duty to raise our children. This means teaching them our values, our customs, and our society along with practical life skills, chores, and more. Furthermore, it's my personal belief that as parents we are to expose them to the world around them, teaching them along the way.

The moment we become parents, we become teachers. We narrate the world around us; pointing out each aspect of daily life and enthusiastically show our children the awesome and wonderful world in which they live. How exciting is it that we get to do this?! We are all the tour-guides to life's beginning. That means you get choose what you teach your child and what fits for your family!

# Narrating Our World

Narration is one of the simplest and easiest forms of teaching and learning. As you give a play-by-play, describing the details of an object or an event, it is easier to deduce what is happening.

For a baby or toddler, they can learn so much through narration. They are introduced to a wide array of terms and vocabulary, all in real-time. This means that a word or an action has meaning and context. Your own thought processes rely on connections and relationships; therefore, teaching your children to make connections in their daily lives is important. For instance, a picture of a toothbrush has no true meaning or impact, especially if the child has never encountered it before. However, teaching children to associate the tooth-brush with the action of brushing and with the nouns mouth, teeth, and tongue, meaning and relationships are derived from narrating that experience. While I do not hate flashcards, worksheets, or printables, I do like to encourage parents to focus on experiences. Even if the experience is reading a book about a faraway place, it fosters an imagination and not rote fact; the same idea applies to using a printable to make a hands-on game. *That* is what tot-schooling is all about - Digging in, exploring, and getting excited to learn! When learning has meaning and a purpose it becomes fun and effortless for both toddler and parent.

# Playing is Learning

One of the greatest gifts of childhood is the ability to be care-free, imaginative, creative, and playful. As a parent you can tap into that innate desire to play and learn from experience. We all learn so much more from fun and engaging moments in our lives. In fact, you can probably think of at least one example of a game in school that helped you remember something. For kids, playing is the epitome of learning.

Tot-school should be about getting dirty, having adventures, and having no boundaries. Play is a non-threatening way to learn and completely exploratory; it indicates that there is no danger and a child may explore freely and creatively. [This means it is also important to have a defined space for learning and playing which we will discuss later in this book.]

Jean Piaget suggests that learning is something that is provoked and not simply spontaneous. This also means that there comes a point, especially in tot-school and pre-school, where activities, play ideas, and crafts become part of the learning process because the basics of the day have already been mastered.

Therefore, for us, we moved into a tot-school routine when my daughter was around 14 months. This was to facilitate learning and exposure to new ideas and concepts beyond her daily life. For you, this may come earlier or later, it just depends on what fits for your family. It also largely depends on the rate of your child's vocabulary and their mastery of basic skills such as crawling, walking, eating, etc..

Every success and failure is a learning opportunity for our kids. As they fall down and get hurt while playing, they learn the protocol as set by your family for how it gets handled. For us, we tell our daughter to pick herself up and dust herself off. We then comfort as needed and narrate what happened. "You fell while you were carrying something heavy". This provides great analysis and a learning opportunity because we can talk about asking for help, carrying a smaller load, or finding a different toy.

Too many parents wait for preschool to teach their kids and they miss out on the fun it is to have a toddler that is ready and willing to learn and the time when their child is still so innocent that the opinions of others don't matter. Embrace their enthusiasm now and help them explore their world and everything that interests them.

## Building Self-Confidence

I believe we are hard-wired as humans to be more self-confident when we know more. Think of a time in a conversation when someone used a word that you had never heard and would have loved to have had a virtual dictionary in your head in the moment. Or think of a time when you didn't know what an entire group of people around you was talking about, you pretended you did, and then it was exposed that you didn't. I am sure that in those moments you felt very small. I know as I think about times like those in my life, I do not feel an inkling of self-confidence and I do feel plenty of embarrassment. Though it's inevitable, I don't want that for my kids. I want them to feel like they can conquer the world! That's not to say they won't fail or experience disappointment, but it is to say that I want to give them the tools to be confident and explore the unknown fearlessly.

Toddlers have very few outside influences in their lives. This means that as they grow and as they learn, they have a pattern that they can expect. For example, do something good, gain praise. Creating that atmosphere as a toddler where learning and playing is encouraged and there is a pay-off (even if only sheer love, attention, and adoration), means creating a pattern of expectation. When we live by patterns we typically are more confident and more certain of ourselves and the outcomes to expect.

If learning is fun and sharing their knowledge is valuable, a toddler is more likely to want to learn and play even more. As a parent, if you do not scold a child for a wrong answer, but encourage what the child does know, it builds more self confidence. For instance, my daughter struggled with the difference between a duck, a chicken, and goose at first. Instead of telling her "no, it's a ____", we would encourage her and say "you're right, it has a beak!" or "it *does* lay an egg, what else lays an egg?".

Learning and playing is also about helping a child discover who they are and what they like. It is about helping them understand society and where they fit in it. For instance, we live in an older neighborhood, where many neighbors do not speak to one another. We however have made it a game to wave to every single car that drives by our house. This builds my daughter's self-confidence and also teaches her social implications of waving and interacting with those around her. We now have neighbors that stop to talk to her and wave just because she did first.

## Getting Started

Though parenting and playing in themselves are part of learning, I hopefully have piqued your interest and you would like to start a more structured form of tot-schooling! I have teamed up with a wonderful group of fellow bloggers that tot-school at home just like we do. Throughout this book, we will demonstrate how we individually implement a tot-school routine at home. Our varying perspectives are what makes this book unique. Every parent can truly tot-school their child; it is about finding what works for your specific needs to fit your family. For instance, my family focuses on being eco-friendly in everything we do and not spending much money. We also value experiences, so our tot school day does not have a set time or quantity of time.

It's a daily part of our lives, even if it is a just a small aspect of our day. Narration truly is a great form of teaching for such a young age; it gives context to actions and involves my toddler in the process. You may find this to be a very useful tool or you may not. Adopt what rings true to you – what you agree with, what seems feasible, and what you are comfortable doing.

Remember that even busy days and sick days present opportunities to learn. Even if it's just about talking about how body parts may hurt and how we help fix them. Lunch might even be different, so chicken noodle soup when sick may be part of that day's learning experience. Your whole life is full of teaching opportunities; training yourself and your children to recognize them is the most important part of tot-schooling! Remember, in the end it's about socialization, self-confidence, vocabulary building, and playing! So let's get started!

**For more from Kara, check out**

http://ALLterNATIVElearning.com

# Scheduling & Planning
## BY ERIN BUHR OF BAMBINI TRAVEL

Browse online or at a bookstore & it will quickly become clear that there are countless approaches to education. The same can be said for planning to educate. Every teacher has their approach that is fine-tuned over time, ever evolving to fit the needs of the children, classroom, and teacher. Below are some suggestions on planning curriculum for toddlers. Consider them, consider your style, and find a way that works for you.

## It All Begins With a Schedule

In the world of Tot Schooling, everything is curriculum. From the moment a child gets out of bed & tries to pull their own pants on to the moment they practice brushing their teeth before bed, they are learning.

Figuring out how the world works. How their body and ideas fit into the world. How they get along with the other people around them each day. This is the curriculum of toddlers and it all begins with a schedule.

Toddlers need routines and schedules to feel secure in their environment. When they can predict from moment to moment and day to day what will happen next they feel secure. This security comes from structure and from a nurturing caregiver. This security allows them to venture out into the world and explore. Start your tot schooling by outlining a schedule. An order to events. Here are a few things to keep in mind:
•Limit transitions: The fewer times you have to ask your child to clean up or move on to something else the smoother your day will flow.

•Schedule meal times and diapering/toileting times at intervals that meet their needs predictably.

•Allow for large chunks of uninterrupted play: try for at least an hour or more a day of time where you are not interrupted a toddler at play.

•Schedule daily gross motor time. Whether it is a trip to a playground, running around the backyard, or marching around with instruments, toddlers need to move and preferably outside.

## Curriculum

Toddler curriculum works best when there is something to get excited about. Consider having a theme, a topic, or something to make everything else relevant. There are two basic ways to get started. One is to have a set curriculum. You have topics that you plan to address. For example, families in September, farms in October, trucks in November, etc. The second is an emergent or project based approach. This involves being in more of a constant state of planning and evolving. Toddlers follow their interests and developmental goals are weaved into those ideas. Some believe strongly in one approach or the other, some people dance somewhere in the middle. The type of approach that suits the needs of each parent, teacher, child, and setting will vary. You need to choose something with which you feel comfortable. Either way, I suggest starting with one topic at a time. A topic you choose (maybe trucks) or a topic your child chooses. From there you can begin to plan.

### Starting Big

Planning begins by looking at the big picture. What are the big themes of the topic? What major skills is my child working on developing right now? Here are some things to start brainstorming on paper:

•Developmental Goals: what is your toddler working towards right now in each area (Cognitive, Language, Fine Motor, Gross Motor, Social/Emotional). There are various developmental checklists that can be helpful here.

•Field Trips: where can you go to see, feel, touch, experience the interest or topic.

•Book Lists: request a stack of books from the library. If your child is old enough, also have your child ask the librarian for book ideas.

•Real Life Examples: similar to field trips, but what real examples can you go to or bring into your environment?

•Sensory Experiences: toddlers are in the sensory stage where they need to get their hands on a topic. Consider all 5 senses. What can they see, hear, touch, taste, and smell? What about this topic's sensory properties might grab their attention? Can clay or other sensory materials be incorporated into their learning?

•Pretend Play: how can they learn about this topic through pretend? Can they dress up like it? Can they engage with a miniature version?

•Materials: what materials do you have on hand that relate to the topic? what else can you bring into the environment by borrowing, creating, or purchasing?

## Week by Week

Set aside some time each week to plan. Perhaps every Friday you sit down with a piece of paper. In general, a toddler schedule is going to look flexible, largely unstructured, and playful. Here are some things to consider on a weekly basis:

•**Materials in the Environment**: Rotate a few toys each week. What is the toddler no longer interested in? Think about your goals for your child. Are they working on learning their colors? What new material could address an interest or support a developmental need? Try to have at least one thing in the environment that addresses each of the following:

•**Fine Motor Skills**: puzzles, lacing cards, things to twist on & off

•**Dramatic Play:** pretend hats, scarves, fabric, pretend people or cars

•**Cognitive:** loose materials to work on shapes, numbers, colors

•**Literacy:** books, objects to feel and name, felt board stories

•**Sensory**: different textured items, water table, light box

•**Creative Materials**: crayons, paper, markers

•**Planned Experiences**: These are activities you plan to have out for your child to do or things you will do together. Again, the majority of a toddler's day should be spent playing. Limit more structured activities to one or two a day. Depending on your space and schedule, these activities might stay out for the whole week or might be available for part of the day. These can include some of the following;

- Cooking Together
- Yoga or other gross movement activity
- Sensory Activities: glurch, clay, music
- Art Activities: painting, collage, drawing
- Field Trips: where are you going this week that relates to your theme?
- Reading: what books are especially wonderful that you want to read aloud?

## Day to Day

Having a plan is great. It makes you feel like you know what to expect. The wonderful and terrifying thing about toddlers however, is that you never know what to expect. Young children have a charming and startling way of surprising you no matter how long you have worked with them. Your plan for the week is great, but *expect* that not everything is going to follow your plan. Your toddler that loved trucks yesterday might discover a love of ducks today. A toddler that sits attentively for ten books in a row one morning might bounce constantly later that same day with an unceasing need for motion.

Watch how they play with materials, ask them questions, listen to their conversations with peers or siblings. Read books and listen to their questions. Use these observations and questions to direct where you go next. If things don't go as you expected, take a deep breath and accept that toddlers are learning what they need to know at their own pace and in their own time. Tomorrow you can go back to the drawing board and make a new plan.

**For more from Erin, check out her site**
http://www.bambinitravel.com/

# Learning by Theme

## BY KARA CARRERO OF ALLTERNATIVELEARNING

## How to arrange your "curriculum"

Learning does not have to be intensive, it just has to be meaningful. Therefore, tot-school curriculum should be fun and it should be new. When those little eyes are absorbing everything around them, it is important to engage that curiosity and willingness to learn and participate. Therefore, my personal opinion is that tot-school ideas and curriculum should be set up and grouped by themes. In separating your weeks and/or months into themes, your child has the ability to learn and play with a particular concept and then move on without it becoming mundane. Themes also provide flexibility. Focusing on shapes for a week or two does not mean that you will never talk about shapes again. *Of course you will discuss shapes again! They're everywhere!* It just means that you have a main focus so that your child also understands the concept.

Our brains work in terms of relationships like understanding that all breeds of dogs are still dogs or that a cow goes "mooo"; they are all memories based upon associations. This means themes also help form connections and lasting memories for our toddlers.

## Vocabulary

Vocabulary is crucial for learning and development because it is broken into four distinct categories – listening, speaking, reading, writing. This means the learning process is truly a life-long endeavor, as babies are building vocabularies just by listening. It  also means that a person cannot skip from listening to reading without intermediate steps. Planning out and dividing units by theme allows children to build  a vast vocabulary. From knowing animals of the jungle to understanding body parts, vocabulary leads to a greater understanding for a toddler and it also is a stepping stone towards later, more traditional, schooling.

## Exposure to a Diverse World

Investigating diversity in nature, in people, and in places helps develop an understanding of opposites, of similarities, and builds overall awareness, vocabulary, and even empathy towards others. As people, when we begin to understand our world a bit better, we engage in it more and dig deeper into those topics that become passions later in life. The idea that a toddler could grow up to be absolutely anything they want to be all revolves around what they are exposed to in life. The dream of being a ballerina never occurred to the child that had not danced or attended the Ballet. The aspiration of being a doctor never occurred to the child that hadn't been cared for, or better yet, cared for someone else. Ultimately, we are the vehicle by which our children learn about different types of people, the beauty of unique places, and just the vast world around us. Being a part of a digital and global age, it is becoming ever-more important for even toddlers to understand life outside of who they are and where they live.

**For more from Kara, check out**
**http://ALLterNATIVElearning.com**

# Rate of Development

BY KATIE T. CHRISTIANSEN OF PRESCHOOL INSPIRATIONS

The tot years are such a magical time to watch children grow and develop. Oftentimes, it feels as though they are learning new skills every week. As each child matures and develops, milestones will emerge at different times for every little one. These new skills will also look different from one child to the next. A child who spends more time being active and is more interested in running and moving many times will start talking later than the child who seeks out social interactions constantly and spends their days practicing word sounds. Of course there are exceptions to this as well.

The best way that parents can partner with children during these milestones is to enjoy these special moments and put away the ever so tempting "over-analytical microscope." Here are three tips to keep in mind during your child's development.

## Repetition shows growth

Oftentimes, a child engages in an activity such as emptying the contents of a bucket or basket, over and over again. It may seem that very little is being gained from an activity such as this. However, repetition is foundational to the learning process, and while it might look as though the child is just doing one thing, there are numerous skills going on. A child gleans so much more information than we give them credit for. The process of repetition gives the child the ability to take in new information, to observe, and to gather conclusions about their actions.

## Focus on your child's interests

Learning and growing is a natural skill, and the best way that adults can facilitate in a child's development is by following the child's lead. They will naturally work on skills and activities that they are trying to master. Sometimes children work on these skills in their sleep even. As long as children are provided opportunities and loving

19

environments that encourage them to safely explore and discover, you are giving them all the tools they need to progress into the preschool years and beyond.

## Avoid comparison

It is easy to get caught in the trap of comparison. Conversations among parents can often focus on milestones & at which age they were achieved. While these are well meaning or something that is exciting, they can be disheartening & become a false gauge. A child's development is driven by his/her own interests and while one child may naturally love to learn about letters, your child may be fascinated by bugs and nature. Both scenarios are what is best for each child.

Tot years should be cherished and enjoyed! Relish in your child's interests and encourage them in the areas that they seek your help. Above all, trust your child's lead and keep in mind that every child is different and unique.

## For more from Katie, check out:
http://preschoolinspirations.com/

# Environment as the 3rd Teacher

## BY JENNIFER TAMMY OF STUDY AT HOME MAMA

The Reggio-Emilia philosophy created by Loris Malaguzzi is rooted in a respect and reverence for children. Malaguzzi put forth a theory about "the environment serving as the third teacher," which has come to inform and inspire many modern educators. The root of the idea is that the environment is capable of influencing, nurturing, and instructing children in gentle ways, just the same as a teacher would.

This concept is challenging even within a classroom setting, where the primary activity is learning, but the challenge can be even more daunting in the home. Strict budgets, a lack of training, and multiple functions for spaces can all make the task of setting up a truly enriching learning environment overwhelming.

The first thing that must be done is to sit down and be honest about our core believes about children. This makes every other consideration of the space so much easier. Just start writing down ideas and words as they come to you – do you believe children are messy? Do you believe children are capable, or do they always need help? Do you believe children need entertainment, or do they need engagement? What do you think children deserve?

It's completely okay if some of your beliefs about children aren't completely empowering or positive; it's good to be honest & aware of them as they will come up as you start designing and making over your space. For example, if you feel like your kids are always in need of entertainment & aren't capable of entertaining themselves or engaging in activities alone, you might be skeptical about removing entertainment (and possibly technology) from their primary environment. If you believe children are destructive, you *will* have a hard time giving your children access to some objects.

If you root yourself in positive beliefs about children, and are prepared to work against your negative beliefs, you will have the best success in creating an environment that honours the child. (*Do you think that children should be respected and honoured?*)

Before even looking at the playroom, walk through your child's general environment with a critical eye. What does their environment say about them, and about what you think of them? (And if you find that certain aspects of their environment are not ideal, don't feel guilty or overwhelmed! Feel proud that you are identifying issues now and know that you can handle them.)

•Visual clutter distracts the mind, and witnessing a lack of care in the environment can influence children to make similar value judgements. If I'm constantly leaving messes and not cleaning up after myself, why should my child be inclined to?

•Is your space accessible to children, or do they need to constantly ask for help with using the space? Do they have stools where they need them? Are the things that they use regularly meant for little hands? *For example, a stool, lightswitch extender, and easy soap pump or bar in the bathroom can transform hand washing into an independent activity.*

•Do my children have a spot to call their own? Are they truly able to be free in this space? (*For example, if the art table is directly on top of a white carpet, without a drop cloth or doodle pad covering up the floor, are you really going to allow for open exploration?*)

•How do you feel when you look at your child's general environment? Do you think it welcomes children?

•How do you feel when you look at your child's personal environment? Is it reflective of them, their interests, and positive beliefs about children?

Create a game plan to handle your spaces and influences in the environment. If (like me!) you are prone to clutter, create drop zones and figure out how you will be able to clear those drop zones every day.

Next, assess the personal spaces that you have made available for your children and make changes that reflect what you have observed – if there are discrepancies between the environment and your beliefs about children, they should be addressed. For example, if you don't believe children need entertainment, remove things that are overwhelmingly entertaining – televisions, button-and-battery toys that keep going for several minutes after a child has stopped interacting with the toy, etc.

After you have removed everything that is not working in the space, you can start creating! What does your child enjoy? What does your child need help with? What are you constantly intervening to do for your child?

Know that a well prepared environment can take over any task that you used to do, can engage your children in ideas and activities that they previously avoided, and can allow our children to express themselves in ways you may have never thought possible!

If you are intervening often to resolve conflicts, where are the conflicts stemming from? Are there aspects of the environment that contribute to conflicts? Are there things that can be added to the environment to aid in conflict resolution – like a peace corner, or a "talking stick"? Not every solution is going to work for every child, but under the belief that children are capable, we can attempt to create spaces that allow children to work together in solving all kinds of issues – from sibling tiffs to brushing teeth.

Does your child love performing? Could they have a small platform with open-ended "costumes" (like a simple silk scarf) to act upon? Does your child love building yet avoid math? Can you add natural learning opportunities to their block station that will be engaging and appeal to their natural inclinations?

Ensure that any aspect of the environment is made appealing and engaging. A beautiful bookcase is a great start, but children will also need comfortable seating and perhaps a stuffed animal audience to "read to."

When in doubt, opt for soothing and natural influences rather than bright and overwhelming installations. The sensory input that you put into the environment will directly affect how your children interact with it. A circus-like colour scheme might just influence circus-like behaviour! Have you considered how the room smells, the lighting, the textures and temperatures (is that wooden floor too cold or hard on little feet?), and the sounds. Work with what is already naturally occurring in the space to enhance it for the children. Even though it's not as convenient for cooking, I keep my herb plants in the playroom and they add a delicious and natural aroma to the air.

Sometimes, the best playrooms and environments are sparse yet inviting. Trust that you can provide exactly what it is that your child needs from their environment, via easy DIY projects and protecting their safe, nurturing space.

**For more from Jennifer check out:**
http://studyathomemama.ca/

# Defined Play Spaces

## BY MONICA PRUETT OF
## HAPPY AND BLESSED HOME

My firstborn was born at 30 weeks and together, he, my husband, and I spent six and half weeks at the Neonatal Intensive Care Unit (NICU) until he was strong enough to come home. One of the most important things I learned through the experience can be summed up in a single belief expressed by a NICU nurse, "You are your child's greatest advocate. No one will know your child like you will."

If you are reading this book then you already know that it does not require a teaching degree to educate, encourage, and inspire your child- you are your child(ren)'s greatest advocate. Every educator I know agrees that the single most influential and reliable factor in predicting the success or failure of a student is the support and involvement of the parent(s).

Now whether you decide to homeschool or public school your child, preschooling at home is a wonderful way to enjoy the earliest years of your child's life. Developmentally there is so much going on between birth and age six that I dare say you could not fit it all within one book. Parents can have a tremendous amount of influence during these early years. Not only can families dip into math and reading, children can be taught manners, acceptable behaviors, family values, and habits that will set them up for successful living.

In this book, I will share some tips for home set-up, specifically, ways to set-up play spaces and define spaces for learning. These spaces are commonly referred to as "activity centers" or "learning centers."

## Defined Spaces for Learning

Preschool activity centers are centralized areas with a purpose. They are a great way to help young children recognize organization and structure at home or in the classroom.

To create learning centers within your home you'll want to consider your child's interests as well as your available space and budget. In addition, it may be possible to take advantage of activity centers in your community. Playgrounds and libraries are great places to find wonderful learning and activity centers.

This list includes some of the preschool learning centers we use in our home. These organized centers for learning are also known as activity centers and include:

- Circle Time Morning Board
- All Purpose Learning Center
- Art Activity Center
- Kitchen Learning Center
- Reading Center
- Gross Motor Skills Activity Center
- Fine Motor Skills Activity Center
- Dramatic Play Center

The following includes the set-up for each of the above-mentioned activity centers with some money saving tips included. Where applicable, I've included links to blog posts where you can find more information. If you're looking to outfit your preschool set up at home, you will find affiliate links included here for your convenience.

## Preschool Circle Time Morning Board Learning Center

We use a try-fold display board for organizing our learning activities for the day.It's a wonderful tool because it's portable & collapsible. These unique qualities make it a tool that can transform the breakfast area, dining table, or even a coffee table into a mini-classroom.

A Circle Time Morning Board is a great way to introduce the basics - a monthly calendar, planned activities for the day, seasons, tracking weather, basic shapes, colors and numbers, alphabet letters, play games and much more. It's a nice location to introduce any sort of learning activity to young children - if you can make a presentation about a learning topic - it can easily go on a learning board.

We created our learning board using contact paper applied to a tri-fold cardboard display. In addition to displaying learning activities on the morning board, you may want to print out some copies for your child to use. We use stickers, markers, crayons and paint to color our morning board printables. I've also found that blue tack is extremely helpful in teaching my little ones to match numbers and assemble charts.

## All Purpose Activity Center

If you are looking for a set-up that will support many different kinds of activities for play and learning, you'll want to set-up a child-size table and chair set in your homeschool or preschool classroom (or "classroom area). This setup serves many functions. Not only is it great for artwork, writing, reading, and crafts, it's a great place to teach children how to sit down to have a meal, set a place-setting, prepare pretend food & so much more.

## Art Activity Center

Sometimes our table acts as the perfect place for markers, crayons, & colored paints but we absolutely love our stand-up easel. There's something special about painting on the vertical that excites them; my 2 little ones will spend hours painting on our easel if I let them. We also use our easel to learn about letters, numbers, & play games.

**Some tips for arts and crafts activities:**
- Limit the amount of colors and supplies for each child. I usually offer no more than four colors at a time, and only one brush for painting.
- You can make inexpensive painting smocks from kitchen trash bags or you can use store-bought smocks, either way, it's a great idea to teach young children to avoid getting their clothes ruined.
- Teach children early on to wash their hands as soon as they are finished - that way, as they get older, they expect to wash up after playing.
- Use non-toxic washable paints and colors. Young children like to put things in their mouth, up their nose, and in their ears - they are very creative!
- Arts and crafts should be a supervised activity. Paints and glue can easily make it over to the couch, the carpet, leather furniture - you get the idea. It's best to stay close by and provide children with guidance during arts and crafts.

If you'll be creating a bunch of artwork, it's also a great idea to have an art wall or clothesline to hang your child's artwork from. Find a wall in the house not being used and create an art gallery to help your child showcase his or her artwork.

## Kitchen Learning Center

Children will watch Mom and Dad and want to copy what they see. Learning centers that create opportunities for role playing help encourage imaginative play. A Kitchen Learning Center can include a child-sized kitchen or be something as simple as a cupboard in the kitchen with a few non-breakable kitchen tools, measuring cups, spoons, and/or plastic containers inside the cupboard.

Help your child learn how to play "lunch" or "set the table" by playing alongside them the first few times. This helps teach about the functionality of the kitchen or table where they are playing and will enable them to envision role-playing. Once I taught my boys how to "make a sandwich" and "serve drinks", they happily invited stuffed animals and other toys to eat a meal with them. These types of activities encourage imaginative play and help teach important life skills like sharing and hospitality.

## Reading Activity Center

Young children love to explore books. One of the activities my children enjoy is making a trip to the library to pick out books. This encourages a love of reading which is also a love of learning. When you set up your reading activity center, you want to keep all the books at child-height. Teach young children to put books away with the binding out. If you have the resources, create a sitting area near your reading center to encourage young children to sit down and open a book.

## Fine Motor Skills

Just as important as gross motor skills are fine motor skills. Learning how to pinch a pencil, hold a fork, unscrew a small lid, cut with scissors - all are important life skills. Tools that can help children develop fine motor skills include things like puzzles, coloring supplies, and building blocks.

By mixing puzzle pieces from similar wood puzzles, the task of puzzle assembly has become a bit more challenging.  If you have a group of children trying to complete a puzzle, this can also foster communication, sharing, and problem solving.

## Dramatic Play

Playing dress-up, playing with puppets, animating stories with puppet sticks, and acting out stories are all forms of dramatic play. This type of play helps children develop social skills, their imagination, creativity, and freedom to express themselves in a role playing environment.

You can create a theatre from a cardboard box and make inexpensive puppets from paper bags and construction paper. If your child has a favorite character, Google the character and you can often find online sources for free character images that are licensed for personal use. Some of our favorite resources include Sesame Street from PBS online and Disney characters from Disney Junior online.

Even at a young age children will recognize a book by its cover and quickly develop favorites. Since the brain learns language through pattern recognition, reading the same story over and over again to your child can help a child learn how to form words and talk.  To help children learn how to read, point out words as you read them. Patterns help the brain to recognize common sounds, inflection, and emphasis.

## Gross Motor Skills Activity Center

Skills like climbing, walking, and running are gross motor skills.  Some of the best activity centers for enhancing gross motor skills can be found at local parks. Slides, rock wall, ladders, swings, monkey bars and the like are great for teaching young children hand-eye coordination, as well as developing muscular strength. As young children learn how to get around on play gyms, it's important to stay close by and supervise their play. Accidents can and do happen and it's important to keep gross motor skill activity under close watch to prevent injury.

## In Conclusion

There are many wonderful ways to set up and define play spaces for children. You can use shoe boxes to create parking garages and places to park toy cars, create or purchase plastic tools to create a tool box or tool belt, turn old clothing into costume pieces like a cape for Superman, or a drinking straw into a princess wand. There are countless ways to turn almost any space into an imaginary play land for young children.

Don't let your kids have all the fun, join in whenever you can and spend a little time reliving your childhood. A good friend once told me they'd learned the secret to eternal youth - take time out and play like a child *{wink}*.

You are your child's greatest advocate and their most influential teacher. I hope these ideas will inspire you to create play spaces that teach, inspire, and ignite learning and

**For more from Monica, check out:**
http://www.happyandblessedhome.com/

# *Practical Life*
## BY <u>BECKY MARIE</u> OF
## <u>FOR THIS SEASON</u>

## Promoting Independence in your Toddler

When my oldest was a young toddler, we would spend the mornings playing together, then during nap time I would scramble to get all the house hold chores done. One day I realized he could actually help me with things around the house. I started training my oldest when he was close to three, but my other two boys started helping with chores before they could walk. There are many different terms used throughout the various approaches to early childhood education, but all reflect the same desire to promote independence. You will see the terms chores, practical life exercise, self care, and independence used throughout this book, often interchangeably.

## When should you start?

Right away! As a child grows up they will be able to help more and more around the house, but there is no reason to wait to a particular age to start your instruction. Babies can be taught to put toys back into baskets or tubs before they even learn to walk. When a baby is able to sit, you can give them a clean rag to help wash low windows, mirrors, or even the floor. While their efforts probably are not helping you to actually clean anything and they certainly are not helping you do it any faster, you are setting the expectation at a young age that everyone can and will help with chores.

## Chores for Each Age

There are many different age-based chore charts floating around blogs and pinterest, and I think they are great for providing inspiration. An appropriate chore for your child is to observe what they are interested in doing and what needs to get done around the house. For example, when we fold laundry everyone has a job.  My 6 year old can fold and put away almost all of his clothes and help with kitchen napkins and towels.  My 3 year old can fold square washcloths and napkins and match socks.  The 1 year old toddler can help sort clothes into plies and put some things away in their baskets in our closet.  As they each master a task, I introduce a new step.  We work side by side so I can provide corrections if needed and play cheerleader when they get frustrated.

## Set up a Prepared Environment Specifically for Chores

The Prepared Environment is a concept from the Montessori approach to early childhood education.  The term is most often used when showing examples or providing guidance for setting up a learning space.  I think it also extends to the whole house.  If you want your children to complete chores independently, then prepare a working area for them.  Place the items they need for a particular job in an easy to access place at their level.  I keep the kids brooms and dustpans on hooks in our front closet and a basket of vinegar-filled* squirt bottles and rags in the bathroom.  In the kitchen, I moved all our cups and dishes to a low shelf so the boys are able to put things away or set the table without any help.  Take a few moments to observe your child and how they act in the various rooms in your home.  If necessary, move things around to create the opportunity for independence.

*A note on cleaning with vinegar – it is not great as a cleaner in and of itself but it is something I feel very comfortable allowing my young toddler to use.  The boys are responsible for wiping down the bathrooms twice a week.  Once a week or every other week, I deep clean the bathrooms with commercial cleaning products.

**For more from Becky, check out:**
http://www.forthisseason.com/

# Getting Dressed

### BY AMANDA BOYARSHINOV OF
### THE EDUCATORS' SPIN ON IT

## Teaching Your Child to Dress Themselves

Mornings can be hectic. Teaching your toddler how to dress themselves is NOT the fastest part of our morning routine. In fact, it is one of the most time consuming. This skill, however, is a good skill to have. Although many children will be able to dress independently by the age of 3, I start teaching my children how to get dressed on their own at 15 months old. They start to show an interest in getting dressed by putting their arms in the holes, stepping into pant legs, and verbalizing what clothing they want to wear. Teaching toddlers to get dressed on their own gives them ownership over their belongings, allows for fine motor practice, and fosters independence. Admittedly, getting dressed independently is not a time saver, it is, however, a learning experience.

## How to Start Teaching Your Child

As your child starts to show an interest in getting themselves dressed in the morning, start by verbalizing what they need to do. Explain to them that they are old enough to help get dressed in the morning. Use your words to coach them through getting dressed with an adult. A parent may say, *"We set our pants out on the floor with the legs out like this. Then we put one leg in. PULL. Now the other. PULL. That's right. Now stand up and tug the back like this.* {hold your hand with theirs to pull the elastic band over their undergarment."

Soon, you will say, *"Time to get dressed."* and your toddler will sit on the floor in anticipation of putting his pants on. He may even help set his pants out and start to stick a foot inside. At this point, the toddler and parent work together to get dressed.
In a few weeks, or even months, your toddler will be ready to put on his own clothes. Make sure to pick a day where you have extra time and are not rushed. Provide your

toddler with 2 outfit choices and ask them toddler to get dressed. Be there to support them if needed, but let them do as much as they can on their own.

**Best Clothes for Teaching Toddlers to Get Dressed**
   -Ditch the jeans, button up shirts, and tie shoes for teaching toddlers how to dress themselves.
   -Shorts and pants should be loose fitting, so that little hands can tug them over diapered bottoms easily. Check the waistband elastic to make sure it is stretchy enough to fit around their waste, but not stretchy enough to fall off!
   -Make sure that t-shirts have big enough neck holes to stretch easily over heads.
   -Find slip on shoes or easy Velcro shoes.

## Tips and Tricks for Getting Dressed.

1. Have your child sit down on the floor. Have them lay the pants out in front of them. Teach them to put both feet in the legs and yank the pants as high as they can before standing up. Once standing, show them how to reach behind their back to grab the waistband and slide it over their diapers or undies.

2. For shirts, toddlers seem to do best by pushing their head through the neck hole first, then finding the arm holes afterwards.

3. Crocks and slip on shoes are the easiest for young children to put on independently. They are not always the best for running and outside play. We try to have several options of shoes available for our toddler to choose from. Holding the tongue up and sliding a foot in is good tip for getting shoes on. Grabbing by the heels to pull is helpful to get off.

**For more from Amanda, check out:**
http://www.theeducatorsspinonit.com/

# *Potty Training*

## BY ERIN BUHR OF
## BAMBINI TRAVEL

Everything is curriculum when working with young children. Everything. Toddlers need to learn color names and animal sounds, but they also need to learn to set the table, watch the garbage truck, wipe up their spills, and learn how to use the toilet. These things are all part of a toddler curriculum. Toilet training can be stressful for caregivers and children, but when adequately prepared for and done when the child is ready it does not have to be. The success of toilet learning primarily hinges on four things; environment, routine, child preparedness, and a boat load of patience.

## Setting Up The Environment

When your toddler starts to show awareness of toileting, it is a good time to get your environment prepared. This does not mean that your toddler will be in underwear the next day, it just means that you are making the space accessible & welcoming for your child. Here are some things to provide:

- Child sized toilet or child-sized seat on the regular toilet
- Stools for their feet while toileting and for reaching the sink
- Towel on a hook at their height
- Book or two about using the toilet
- Easily and independently removable clothing. (ie. avoid buttons, snaps, and overalls)

## Toileting + Your Schedule

Make time during the day for toileting. The easiest way is often to offer a try at diaper changes. Simply ask "Do you want to try using the toilet?" Yes and no are acceptable answers and make sure not to put pressure on your child. Expect that some days your

Give them space to try and teach them how to wipe, flush, and wash their hands each time. This way, when they are ready they have the skills to be successful and sanitary.

toddler will be interested and some days they will not. With time, if you make toileting part of the routine, it will gradually become something they just do.

When they are successful, acknowledge their achievement in small but excited ways. This can simply be to state "look what you did!" Or if you want to sometimes do more you could try letting them call another parent, send a grandparent a text, or give them a stamp on their hand. There is a fine line between exciting encouragement and overdoing it. You have to figure out where this line is for you. For me, I believe in praising my children but I also want their pride to come from within. I want them to be proud of themselves and for that to be a reward in itself.

## The Underwear Plunge: When + How
It is time to move to underwear when your toddler is;
- Keeping their diaper dry during the day
- Letting you know when they need to go
- Successfully using the toilet
- Interested in wearing underwear

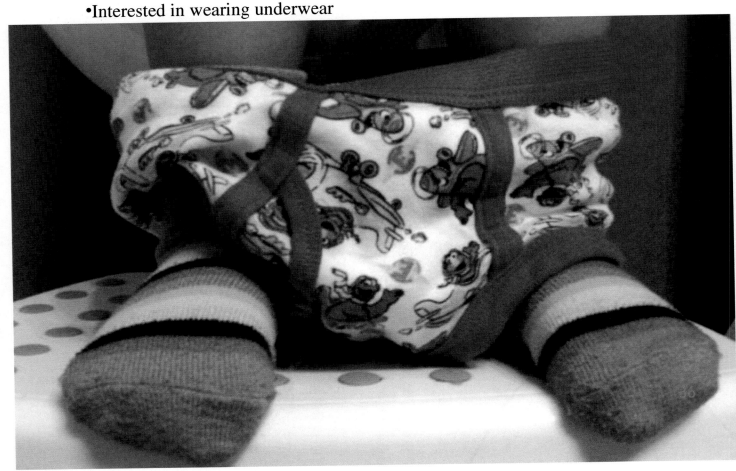

They do not need to be perfect every time, but in order to truly be successful in underwear they need to be capable of doing each of these things most of the time.

It is certainly possible to put your child in underwear sooner and let them run around the house leaving puddles behind them, but this is often where stress plays a role. Regardless of when your child starts wearing underwear, accidents will happen.
However, if you wait until your child is ready they will be successful more often than not. This helps them feel confident and proud about their new skill. A few tips to make the move to underwear successful:

- Remove the diapers. If you will still be using diapers for naps or bedtimes, put them in a different space. Make sure they are out of sight during the day and no longer an option.
- Let them pick out their first set of underwear and make a huge deal about their accomplishment
- Celebrate their successes.
- Calmly involve them in cleaning up messes. Toddlers are able to remove wet clothing, help wipe themselves off, and find dry clothes.

These steps might sound like an over-simplification of the process, but in reality these are the steps. The hard part is the persistence. There will be days when it seems like cleaning up mystery puddles is your new fulltime job, but just like your toddler has mostly mastered walking without running into things and getting food into their mouths independently, this is a skill they will also master. Teaching toddlers is about following their lead, giving them the pieces they need, and supporting them while they put the pieces together. It takes time and patience, but every child will get there in their own way and in their own time.

**For more from Erin, check out:**
http://www.bambinitravel.com/

# *Household Goods*

## BY ENMA EDWARDS OF ADVENTURES OF ADAM

The great thing about Tot-school is that you do not need to spend a fortune to get started. You probably already own many resources that can be used to enhance your child's development. Household goods can be used in a variety of ways and typically the activities do not require any set up time. This means you can get involved in the play straight away.

The majority of children's toys today are all singing and all dancing. The saying "the more a toy does, the less your child has to do" holds true. Typically toys require our children to sit and watch the toy perform which is entertaining rather than educational.

Toddlers are little scientists. They want to investigate how everything works and they do This through 'experiments'. Household goods require your toddler to explore their senses and develop an understanding of the world around them. Household goods can help develop fine and gross motor skills, enhance your toddlers thinking skills and thought processes and help build your child's self esteem as they accomplish new tasks.

Below is a list of household goods and how you could use them. It is not a definitive list and your own imagination and child's development will mean you should be able to think of many more. It is surprising that once you start thinking of household goods in terms of how they can aid your toddler's development you will never see household goods in the same light again.

## Plastic cups

These are great for stacking. How many different ways can your toddler find to stack the cups? They are also great for filling, aiding your child's concept of volume, building towers and knocking them down which will teach your child about cause and effect.

## Plastic bottles

Get your toddler to fill them up with pom poms or pipe cleaners. Watch their concentration as they feed the items through the small hole, practicing their fine motor skill development. Why not place The bottle on top of a mirror and see your child's fascination with the reflections. Small plastic bottles can also be filled with rice, cereal or buttons to create Discovery Bottles. Hide small items inside to create I Spy Discovery Bottles.

## Pots and pans

Attach string to the handles and hang them from a gate, bush or laundry tree. Using a variety of kitchen utensils your toddler will have great fun banging away and creating their own music. They will be experimenting with listening to the different sounds made as each utensil strikes the individual pots.

## Colander

This provides useful sized holes for your toddler to post pipe cleaners or straws through. In the bath it becomes a great drain and in the Tuff Spot it can be used to sieve a variety of items – seeds, small beads, sand and dirt to name a few.

### Clothes pegs & pins

Grab your pegs and let your toddler drop them into different baskets. It's amazing how long toddlers will concentrate on transferring activities. As your toddler moves onto pre-writing skills opening and closing clothes pegs is a fantastic way of developing a pincer grip.

### Containers with lids

Putting lids on and taking them off again helps develop your toddler's muscles. Having different sizes of containers means your toddler has to match them up too. Plastic spice containers work well.

### Cardboard toilet rolls

Use the tubes for giant threading by putting them onto a broom handle. Attaching the cardboard tubes to the fridge door (or a large cardboard box) with cellotape creates a super marble run.

### Masking tape

Create a masking tape car track on your floor. This is great for gross motor skills as your toddler pushes their cars around the cityscape. Or place layers of masking tape in different directions on a baking tray. Your toddler will use their fine motor skills to try and peel off the tape

**For more from Emma, check out:**
http://adventuresofadam.co.uk/

# *Books*

## BY <u>MONIQUE B</u> OF <u>LIVING LIFE & LEARNING</u>

Reading books with your toddler is a great way to instill the love of reading at a young age. This is the time to make reading fun and exciting so that they will grow up to love reading books themselves.  Books introduce new vocabulary and allow your discuss pictures and concepts that are not present in everyday life. I don't live on a farm so I wouldn't use farm vocabulary but I'm sure my toddler would love to read about different farm animals.

## Take it slow

I do not think it is possible to hand your child a book on the first try and have them listen and sit through the entire book.  I know that my toddler spent  a lot of time just touching them and chewing on them before they realized it was meant for reading.
I urge you not to rush into reading books because you do not want them to hate it, rather you want it to be a good experience. It is not fun to do something that you are forced to do.

I would set the book out and let my child explore and then if they wanted to know what was in the pictures, we'd read it and talk about the pictures in the book. I didn't always stick to what was written because sometimes they weren't interested in that and we more engaged with something else on the page. I didn't hurry to go on to the next page but we sat and talked about the book and its pictures and I just followed their lead.

This usually gets easier with toddlers that have older siblings because they see their brother or sister reading and want to do the same. They also enjoy choosing their own books instead of having to listen to their siblings  selection.

41

## Set a routine

I make sure the books become a part of our daily routine. We always read in the mornings while the boys are working on their independent studies (we are homeschoolers). This ensures that we have some quiet time and it gives us time to read alone together. We always read before bed as well.

We do it every night and it happens every day along with a bath and brushing your teeth. I make sure that I have enough time for our nightly routine. It has become such a habit that my toddler refuses to go to bed without a book.

## Activities

Books are a great jumping board to other activities, you can incorporate crafts and activities that go along with the story to bring it alive. This extends the story even more, you can create paper crafts, salt dough projects, sensory bins or even snacks. It's a great way to discuss what your are working on and relate it back to the book that you read with your child.

We made salt dough fossils using my son's dinosaur toys after we read a dinosaur book. My boys love dinosaurs so my daughter loves them as well. She's loves taking out the toys and showing me how the dinosaurs eat and play. It's great to watch them make the connections between what we are reading and what they've learned.

### Follow their lead

Don't rush to finish the book, the joy is in experiencing the book with your child. If you're child isn't ready to turn the page and go on that relish the fact that they are really enjoying that page. Let them tell you when they are done reading so that you keep it a light and engaging activity that ends on a high note.

### Visit the library

Make a trip to the library a fun field trip. I love the library, you get to enjoy all the books you can and it's all free (minus late charges). Where else can you go and have your child select from hundreds of books. You allow them to choose for themselves and you may find a surprise reading selection that you would never have thought of yourself.

### Great books

Expose your child to a variety of books, large colorful picture books about people, animals, and places. Don't confine them to what you think they will like based on sex. My daughter loves to read books with cars and trucks because she loves playing with her brothers toys.

**For more from Monique, check out:**
http://www.livinglifeandlearning.com

# Craft Supplies

## BY BIRUTE EFE OF PLAYTIVITIES

Doing crafts and other cool stuff with kids is not only super fun but also very beneficial for them. But it doesn't mean that you need to rush to the art supply store and load the cart with fancy supplies. Actually you probably already have everything in your house. Look around and your crafting supplies are in your pantry, kitchen and the trash bin.

The most common craft supplies that we find around the house and use are:
- Cardboard boxes
- Shoe boxes
- Plastic bottle and plastic bottle caps
- Old pieces of broken toys
- Carton milk containers
- Plastic yogurt lids
- Toilet paper/ towel paper rolls
- Old umbrella
- Socks
- Old magazines and newspapers
- And more!

Here are my top ideas on where to get supplies and materials for your toy making projects and other crafts. P.S. Get ready to save a lot of money and get addicted to it.

1.  If you want to load up on toy making and craft supplies faster it's a great idea to hit the second hand stores like Goodwill or some garage sales. You will be surprised at what people throw away and you can have it for just pennies.

2.  I suggest you make good friends with local shoe stores because they will be

providing you with some of the best stuff for free. Shoe boxes!

3. Always keep an eye on other stores that throw away big cardboard boxes, wrapping paper, bubble wrap, plastic cell phone packing boxes. These are all ideal for your projects. Don't be shy to ask manager when you go into the store.

4. I also have asked friends and family who live near by to not throw away glass, paper or plastic milk containers, plastic bottle caps, big cardboard boxes, bubble wrap or anything else they think I would find a great use for.

5. When I need project that requires a piece of wood (for a swing, play kitchen or even a toy truck) I go to my local lumber store. Not the big chain, but small family operated one, where all they do is just cut wood. Ask them if they have any scraps they don't need anymore. You will be surprised at what they will give you. For a smile  a big thank you.

6. At the end of the year I ask my daughter's preschool teacher if she has any art supplies that she is going to throw away. Empty acrylic paint containers, even markers that don't write anymore could be a big treasure.

7. Check your local paper recycling bins, especially the ones near bookstores. The amount of quality colored paper (from magazines) for your projects you will find in there will surprise you.

8. Ask a local restaurant staff if they could save for you things that they would normally throw away like coffee cans, cardboard rolls, paper canisters, even the egg cartons.

9. Visit fabric store and ask if they have any scraps of fabric that they don't have use for.

10. Look for free or very cheap things for your projects online. Craigslist has many ads where people would give away stuff for free if you just pick it up from their house.

**For more from Birute, check out:**
http://playtivities.com/

# Developing Attention

### BY MELISSA MISRA OF SWAMI MOMMI

## Babies and Toddlers and Attention Skills

Starting at the beginning…how can we start our kids out from birth on the road to good attention? How can we help our little ones be focused big ones? Taking stock of our own attentional habits is a good place to start. Creating environments where our babies can thrive comes in a close second to making a difference in our kids' attentional development.

## Nutrition

Babies can benefit from many things we as parents do. From birth, we know that supporting brain health is often most simply done by providing good nutrition. It is very important to understand that the stomach links directly to the brain. The stomach makes up the enteric nervous system, and it is crucial in making neurotransmitters that are important for attention and mood, much like the brain.

Additionally, the gut is the first place where a child's immune system is turned on. Traveling through the birthing canal helps the baby ingest beneficial bacteria from the mother to turn on immunity. Immunity secures the future gut health over the long term, and overall health as well.

A balance is also necessary. In talking about children, sugar is one of the main culprits that rocks the once-nutritious apple cart. Years ago, sugar was a special treat, a few times a week if a kid was lucky. In the 70's and 80's, when the US government allowed food manufactures to legally market directly to kids, we saw a tremendous increase in

47

food placement ads directed at kids. Most of the foods were sugar-rich and nutrient-low. Now sugar and processed food are staples for most daily meals for kids.

As parents, we have two challenges; first to locate both healthy and convenient options in grocery stores, and then to communicate to our kids that just because a superhero is on the bag, the food is not necessarily filled with good things.

At the baby age, we can attend to our babies needs, without the burden of explaining superhero food labeling; however, we also have the breast food/best food dilemma. Breastfeeding is great in that it helps the gut turn on the immune system by providing antibodies from the mother directly into the babies' digestive systems. GREAT! But moms often work outside the home, and in the USA, women have very little maternity leave. If a employer doesn't allow for pumping breaks, or a mom can't afford to buy a $200 breast pump (really?) what is a mom to do? Some moms are able to figure out a way to breastfeed, but others move on to formula. Formula is great for nutrients...AND refined sugar. Lots of it. Refined sugar is banned in all formula in some countries in Europe...but it is in almost all formula in the US. Makes me wonder what is the most nutritious formula. I was lucky to find a formula with an alternate sugar source when we needed to supplement with formula, but we paid several dollars more per container.

## Sensory
Sensory soothing also assists babies and toddlers in self-regulation, an important component to attention. They have a better chance to self-calm and soothe themselves when their general environment is characterized by safety and support. This basic idea, of trusting their environment, helps them to lay down brain architecture that supports development. Chronic stress, on the other hand, does the opposite, with milestones not being met as a result. Research presented by The Center for the Developing Child at Harvard University supports the correlation between toxic stress and developmental delay. So creating homes with positive family relationships that are supportive for the baby are the first steps in laying down brain connections that support attention. Simply put, the less stress in a home, the more attention skills develop.

## Habits
As kids get a little older, we have more time to observe our own habits related to attention. Although seemingly still very young, our toddlers will begin to observe and

copy our habits. It's a critical time to make sure their environment is set up to facilitate attention. So let's ask ourselves; how much time are we distracted from our kids? Do we look them in the eye, or sideways as we check our messages on our phone? Also, what media is distracting our kids? Auditory and visual media affect attentional skill development significantly, so it's time to think about how much media time your kids are getting on a daily basis.

This total includes music, T.V., video games, computers and mobile devices. What is the total for each toddler? What is the total for the family as a whole? The higher the total media time, the lower the total sensory and motor and social developmental time. So the lower the total media time, the better. If you think your child might be behind in technology as a result, I can assure you that the technology is only going to get easier to use, and what we are using now will be outdated. By the time you child has good attention skills, they will be even more prepared to jump on the trend of media, whatever that shall be in the future.

I recently had the opportunity to talk with a computer game developer while sitting at the same table at a recent wedding. He graduated from a highly ranked University and worked for a prominent gaming company. I asked him if he was seeing kids' video games being made that were interested in teaching developmental skills. He said that the main industry goal is to make a profit, and that educational games didn't bring in big returns. Consideration for kids' developmental futures is actually not a priority. He said the industry was more about getting the kids hooked & wanting more video games.

Working with attentional skills and brain development for over 15 years, I understand that the format for media is often designed to influence addiction as well. The constant frame changes present in our current video formats trains the brain to change focus every 1-2 seconds. This is detrimental for developing brains. It lays down architecture that decreases long term attentional skills. Additionally, the executive function centers of the brain are off, and these are the ones that allow for sustained attention, task completion, and problem solving. Video games are similar. In France, for example, no children under the age of 3 are to watch TV. Why? Research study after research study has found that media use at early ages has a significant negative effect on speech skill development and motor learning. In the US, the American Medical Association recommends no TV viewing for kids under the age of two, but profit-driven media companies market their wares to parents who actually are told it will enhance their toddlers' environment that your toddlers will love, and will hopefully provide parents with time to make dinner or take a break when necessary.

## Top 10 List for Parenting an Attentional Toddler/Child

1. Un-plug media for toddlers and young children, and create a time and space for adults to check media when children are not around. Use tools such as a smartphone to connect with other, as a way to model connection, not addiction.

2. Create a child-safe play space that is neat and more "low" stimulation than "high" stimulation. Visually busy walls in classrooms decrease attention in students. Make your home well organized with bins, and shelves where clutter and toys can be put away.

3. Set up toys and activities that are easily accessible so kids can get them on their own. Gross motor activities like indoor bowling, sit-and-spins, and other indoor-outdoor safe games are idea for this age.

4. Select and provide toys that encourage creativity such as building and problem solving construction games. The younger the child, the bigger the blocks.

5. Rotate toys every 2 months or so to keep the toys interesting. Use big bins to keep them orderly and easily stash-able each month. Kids will love to pick their own games and toys, as choice and curiosity rule!

6. Sensory games, toys and activities that focus on physical touch. Soft toys, pom-poms, goo, building pillow forts, getting covered in pillows (safely) and playing games of tickle, tag and HUG! The touch sense is what needs stimulation at this stage of development the most.

7. Happy and joyful play with positive words and encouragement. Laying down basic neurons for successful feelings and fun play will come in handy when they get older and bigger challenges arise. When a child likes to work thought new experiences with their parent, they have a life-long support right from the start. They will be braver and more willing to try things given a strongly connected parental relationship.

8. Kids crave limits. Working with kids showed me that firm and gentle limits win the kids over every time. Following firm limits with positive and specific

praise makes kids feel proud and able to self-regulate. They know that, given certain limits, they can control themselves. As long as the parent is safe, meaning that they (the parents) are not hitting or yelling in the home, and are providing food, clothing and safety, kids trust the parents' rules are in their best interest. If the kids can follow these limits, they feel uber safe.

9. Use puppets! It sounds strange, but emotional regulation helps attentional skills. I have had kids tell my puppets things they would never have told me otherwise. Hard emotions are easier felt and processed when aided by a fluffy puppet. I have had kids tell my puppets they didn't want to be on their ADD medicine, just because the puppet was "acting" hyperactive and that maybe "the puppet needed some medicine". Your kids will totally dig puppets, and even more the sillier you get!

10. Sit and read books, for at least 20 minutes every day. Make sure the pictures are of good artistic quality if you are doing picture books. The more realistic the pictures the better. As your toddler grows they will notice more and more details in the pictures. As you begin reading more and more words, your child will begin following the basic words and develop eye-motor skills. Finally, the attentional head/neck position they will use for the rest of their life is the exact position for reading a book. The position of head tilted forward and down is the position that facilitates attention for learning. The positional system in your inner ear knows this, and it's important to develop brain neurology i n this position.

**For more from Melissa, check out:**
http://swamimommi.com/

# Purposeful Play Time

BY **KIMBERLY HUFF** OF

**NATURAL BEACH LIVING**

One of the many things I am passionate about is purposeful playtime with children. At the earliest stages in life, babies are growing, changing, and learning at a rapid speed. So why not maximize their potential by guiding them in a fun gentle way? With purposeful play, children are learning to share, develop better language skills, and they are also working on dexterity by holding and maneuvering their toys. Play truly is the best foundation to prepare children in early childhood for success in the future.

One of the quotes and theories I always enjoy is from Jean Piaget. He said "Play is the work of children." I love how his theory talks about how children over twelve months are like young scientists and as they develop, their creativity and imagination bloom.

Now, of course, there are several different types of play that are wonderful for children, I'm not saying that purposeful play should happen all of the time. In fact, I believe children need every type of play to learn, and thrive as they grow. Free play and child-led play are definitely necessary. They help build confidence by allowing the child to explore and engage in new experiences.

So let's talk about what play is. Play is enjoyable, play is something without goals that needs to be met, and play is spontaneous. Child-led play is where the child is able to explore and discover the world on his own, in a safe environment, of course. He is able to find and figure out what he is interested in playing with on his own. This is a perfect time for you to observe your child. See what he chooses, listen to him play, talk with him, without making it a lesson, and just enjoy the time.

Purposeful play is a little different than child-led play. The definition of Purposeful is intentional, or significant. Therefore , with purposeful play, you are setting up an area with the intention to teach while playing. Now, when I use the word teach, I don't mean you are standing up telling your child things you want remembered. Not at all. By merely talking with your child and engaging him in conversation while playing, you are teaching. Language development is huge for toddlers. The more you talk to them and play with them, the more they learn.

An example of purposeful play could be, while your child is taking a nap, set up a special rainbow play area in the middle of your room. Choose a favorite book on colors, a couple of favorite dolls, a rainbow streamer, rainbow stacker, or some blocks. This is an invitation to play. Your tot will see that invitation and their eyes will light up.

They will be excited to explore what you have set out for them. As you can see, you can easily pick out a few things that you have already and use a theme to set up an area that looks inviting to your child's eyes. The day we did this activity we must have spent an hour telling her dolly the colors. Stacking up the rainbows in different ways. Hiding the pieces under the chair and under her play silk, reading her color books, and just enjoying ourselves. All of this play while learning and working on so many different skills that toddlers need. This would be considered purposeful play because you set it up. You thought about how you could use a few items to have fun, while you also talked and taught your child.

The toddler years are a time of great development, probably for both you and your tot. The key is to remember you are your child's first role model, first teacher, and first playmate so make it fun, and make it purposeful.

**For more from Kimberly, check out:**
http://www.naturalbeachliving.com/

# Free Play

### BY <u>MELISSA MISRA</u> OF <u>SWAMI MOMMI</u>

## Where Memories and Fun are Created!

In toddlers' development, sensory play and gross motor play go hand in hand. When these two forms of play are allowed to grow into an organic activity, where the kids determine how the play is going to go, Free Play is born.

Free Play is where kids get to use their own creativity! It's where they grow their own confidence in initiating, planning and completing tasks. The results, whether successful or not, lead to learning. Free Play results in learning that is not prescribed. It therefore can lead parents to learn a lot about their own child's interests and personality. *A toddler can turn into a newborn again, a pepper can be a red monster with black bean eyes, and a box of dirt can be a small garden for a little farmer.*

In warm climates gross motor play can easily be done outdoors. In cooler climates, indoors might be better. Regardless, setting up the scene for success is the first step. Safety first. Then think of materials that might warrant good gross motor and sensory play. Outdoors, it's pretty simple, especially if you live near the park or the woods. Kids can find materials and assign their own meanings to them. A Stick could be a kings' scepter, a leaf could be a plate, or a string could be a snake. Kids do well with free play when the expectation for "Free Play" is set. And setting the expectation is quite simple. I usually use the words "Go Play, Have fun!". However, to help our little ones really get the idea of free play, I suggest getting toddlers into a routine of playing this way. On the flip-side, If toddlers are provided from sunrise to sundown with entertainment-based play, Free Play can be difficult.

For example, let's say a toddler first wakes in the morning to play with several push-button toys. These are the ones that song or have a crazy visual result. After breakfast, the toddler watches 2 videos, each 30 minutes long. Next the parent takes them to a story hour where they are entertained for 45 minutes. After lunch, they watch another video. They take a nap, to wake to a bit of iPad video game fun. Dinner is next, right before they roll into their evening routine, a routine with very little time for variation.

Now, routine is good. It's the need for "down time" that needs to be, dare I say it, scheduled more frequently. As parents, we have so little "down time" ourselves! Well, I am of an age that I can still remember when I would have "down time" as a child. Even as an adult, I let myself have this luxury. I do nothing, absolutely nothing. But, as a child, I rarely did nothing. Instead I played. I played whatever in the world I wanted.

Today we call kids engaging in "down time" as "Free Play". And it's important. Let's make sure we do more than let our toddlers use down time to watch TV or play video games. I suggest we turn off the devices, and let the kids entertain themselves.

If you are still not convinced, let me point you in the direction of Peter Gray. He is a researcher who has been studying kids and how they learn and play for decade. In his new book, <u>Free To Learn: Why Unleashing The Instinct to Play Will Make Our Children Happier, More Self-Reliant, and Better Students for Life</u>, as well as in his recent TED talk, Gray makes a case for the much-needed increase in free play. Kids get little down time with days filled with too much structure and being over-scheduled.

Gray points out that it is in Free Play that kids really learn. They learn in ways that don't let them forget. Free Play lets them learn in ways that make them feel happy and self-sufficient. It creates those wonderful kid memories we adults go to when we are stressed. The feelings of comfort and warmth and being loved for who you are, not what you do.

Kids need these experiences, and Gray's research shows that kids that have more "Freedom to Learn" are happier, all the way into adulthood. Gray highlights that kids that have less free play have greater incidence of issues such as anxiety and depression. If we as toddler parents think that more early learning classes, only structured play, and educational-based toys are the way to go, all we need to do is balance things a little. Give 50% more "Free Play" and your toddler will thrive! This is not to say that there is no room for clear limits, safety considerations, and appropriate routine. It is a balanced mix of all these things that facilitates great toddler Free Play.

# Top 10 ways to create great "Free Play".

1. Less is More. If you as a parent do nothing but sit back and relax, you got it.
2. Set the scene so sensory items are toddler safe. Make sure that gross motor items are baby/toddler proof. You can't be too careful.
3. Rotate materials every 1-2 months so they are always interesting. I use a 2 month rotation system that uses big bins for easy switching.
4. Start by setting any limits for the play space. If your toddler is not to leave the yard, or go beyond a certain point, set up the limit as soon as you realize it is necessary. All safety issues should have a limit designated, so they can be creative while not having to be reminded of their limits. This builds listening abilities, but as always, never leave your toddler unattended.
5. Google the words "Adventure Playground Europe Pictures" and you will see that there is really very little set-up needed for gross motor play. Gross motor adventures are really fun if filled with stuff you might just be giving to goodwill! These outdoor adventure parks have old tires, old chairs, old grills, etc. The kids love them. Might not be real pretty, but remember they are temporary.
6. Relax. It will feel strange. Ease into it.
7. Let your kids lead.
8. Play if they ask you to join in; don't just direct. You might be asked to be a firefighter, a cook or a dinosaur veterinarian. Have fun!
9. Allow satisfaction to come over you. Your toddlers are developing lasting memories which they will relate back to as adults in times of difficulty or stress.
10. IF you see your kids being creative, tell them. IF you see them initiating new ides, tell them. Whatever they specifically did that was good, let them know that you think they did it well. They will be more apt to take risks in ways that will help them learn more the next time they get a chance for some "Free Play."

**For more from Melissa, check out:**
http://swamimommi.com/

# Sensory Skills for Tots

## BY HEATHER GREUTMAN OF GOLDEN REFLECTIONS BLOG

Sensory activities with toddlers can be a little tricky since they like to put most things in their mouths!

But before I give you some ideas of sensory activities for your toddler, let's take a brief look at what sensory activities are. **A sensory activity is anything that involves the 5 senses (taste, touch, smell, hearing, sight) and also the vestibular or proprioception systems.**

If you aren't sure what vestibular or proprioceptive input is, here is a quick description.

The vestibular system is located in the inner ear and has to do with balance. The key with vestibular movements is getting the head into as many different positions or planes as possible since that is what activates the various receptors in the inner ear. Jumping, swinging, rolling, hanging are usually associated with vestibular because of the head position.

Proprioceptive input is being able to know where your body is in space and where your limbs are in relation to your body. Muscle planning, grading muscle movement, being able to move your arms and legs without necessarily looking at them all falls under proprioception. Pushing, pulling, jumping, big heavy work movements can all be considered proprioception. Proprioception input is located in the large muscle groups and the spine.

Most people associate the 5 senses with sensory activities. So if you do a search on Google or Pinterest for sensory activities, you will usually find things that are messy, different textures, sounds, colors, smells etc. Usually proprioception and vestibular input are associated with gross motor play, but it is all still sensory input!

Here are some fun ways you can make sure your toddler is exposed to as many different sensory experiences as possible:

- Take a hike
- Wade in a creek or stream
- Visit a herb garden or grow your own
- Grow you own garden
- Take music lessons
- Play music (a variety of styles and genres including classical)
- Include them in cooking or food preparation (if you have picky eaters, this is also a great way to involve them with cooking to encourage them to try the food they prepared).
- Playing on a playground
- Rolling down a hill
- Swinging

I also love to include sensory bins or baskets. I usually set them up in a theme and they always include a sensory base of some kind. All you need is a container, I usually use a plastic bin or tub. Then fill it with your base and include items that the child can dump, pour, mix, and play with in the sensory base. Some simple sensory bases could include:

- Cornmeal
- Couscous
- Beans
- Lentils
- Shaving cream
- Pom-poms
- Sand
- Water
- Dirt
- Noodles (dried or cooked)
- Rice (colored, brown, or white)

Of course, do not use a base that a young child could potentially choke on. Also include items that your child can safely play with and never leave them alone while playing with a sensory bin.

When my daughter was putting a lot of things in her mouth, I stuck to bases that were edible or safe for her to have in her mouth. We used cornmeal and noodles mainly. Then as she got older, I started adding different bases, with supervision.

Also a couple tips for cutting down on the mess inside. You can do sensory activities in the bathtub or set up a child's swimming pool indoors (with no water in it) so that the sensory base is contained. If you are using a tub or a bin, place a blanket or trash bag under the bin. You could also use the kitchen sink or bathroom sink with a stool so that your child can reach.

Once you get the hang of setting sensory activities up for your child, it will become easier and you can start to come up with your own combinations of activities based on your child's interests!

**For more from Heather, check out:**
http://goldenreflectionsblog.com/

# *Music*

## BY <u>ASHLEY FRATELLO</u> OF <u>ONE MINDFUL MOM</u>

Can you think of a day in your existence where you heard no sound? No thoughtful humming, tapping toes, rustling leaves or laughter? Believe it or not, these components of everyday living are not only considered musical, but also a very important part of the development for a child.

Including music in your household can have a positive effect on your toddler's learning years, since it nurtures many developing skills at a very young age. Language development, socialization, emotion regulation, motor skills, creative expression and self-confidence are all fostered by musical experiences.

Music is made up of several basic elements that are organic to the world: pitch, rhythm, dynamics, tonality and tempo. Woven together, they create both simple and complex masterpieces that can be fit for the opera, or even your very own backyard.
If you are reluctant because you think you aren't the next up-and-coming pop star, don't worry! Your toddler won't judge. Just remember that music can be included in everyday activities, using objects you can find around the house and a little bit of imagination. Here are several entertaining activities that introduce musical concepts to your family:

## Pitch

Pitch is the highness or lowness of a single note. Think of a piano – the more you move to the right, the higher the pitch becomes. The farther you travel to the left, the lower the notes become. Fill several cups with varying amounts of water. Using an object, such as a pencil or a craft stick, tap the cup and listen to the "tone" it makes. Match your voice to the tone by singing it to the words "la la la". If you need to search for the pitch with your voice, go right ahead! Sliding up and down with your vocal cords is a silly exercise, so encourage your child to do the same.

Adding pitch to your speaking voice is also a great way to attract your toddler's attention. Using one note per word, you can sing short suggestions, such as, "Say hello to daddy", or "Time to eat dinner!" This introduces melody, as well as encourages language development and music composition.

## Rhythm

Do you have any empty oatmeal containers lying around? How about plastic bottles? Pots and pans? Maybe cardboard tubes? These household objects can be used as percussion instruments, which are perfect for exploring a steady beat and rhythm. Every song has a steady beat – something you can comfortably clap your hands to. Within those beats are other sounds that fit in, which is called the rhythm. To introduce this theory, tap a beat with your instrument and sing a familiar nursery rhyme with your child. Guide her hands as she follows along. You can also play with the rhythm by tapping one beat per syllable in the song's lyrics.

## Dynamics

I am sure your child knows the difference between being loud and quiet, right? Well, put those musical concepts to good use by reading a book at different volumes. Introduce a quiet passage by saying the word "piano" (pee-yah-no), hunching down and making your body small. Next, say the word "forte!"(for-tay), raising your voice to speak loudly and sitting up tall. You can continue working on dynamics while singing in the car, or even playing with the volume on the radio by asking your child, "Can you make the song sound forte? How about piano?".

## Tonality

Pick your child's favorite book – either the same one from before, or a different one altogether. While you read the book, play with your voice so it matches a specific character. Is there a mouse in the story? Make your voice high and squeaky. What about an ogre? Deepen your tone and speak slowly. Encourage your child to make the same noises, and applaud their character choices. Have a conversation with the family in the same voices, or introduce new ones, like a monotone donkey, or a sing-songy fairy.

## Tempo

Tempo is the musical element of speed within a song. Take your child outside and run at a fast pace, saying the word "allegro!" which means "go fast" in the language of music. Switch to slower pace while saying "largo!". You can also play with the pitch of your voice to match the movements to emphasize the meaning of the word.

When the basic elements are combined, that is when the magic happens. Take these activities and add them to your day, or make up your own to support your toddler's skills and overall music appreciation experience. Happy Playing!

**For more from Ashley, visit:**
http://onemindfulmom.com/

# *Fine Motor Skills*
## BY HEATHER GREUTMAN OF
## GOLDEN REFLECTIONS BLOG

What you may not realize is that fine motor skills start to develop almost at birth. By 3 months old, a baby is learning how to reach out and grab a hold of items that interest them. This is the beginning of fine motor skills.

Fine motor skills also develop in a age appropriate sequence! The list is really extensive, so I will just be sharing the typical fine motor development from ages 9 months 3 years old with you. If you would like to see the complete list, you can check out the resource links below.

## 6-9 months old
- Begins to grasp & hold onto objects
- Uses a raking grasp to move objects with fingers
- Looking for one object while holding another
- Pokes at objects using their index finger
- Take objects to their mouth
- Explore textures and sensory input with their mouths
- Begin to hold their bottle
- Squeezes objects with their fist
- Play with their own hands

## 9-12 months old
- Begins to feed themselves finger foods
- Will turn pages in a book a few pages at a time
- Begins to put small objects in a cup or container

•Pincer grasp develops (using index finger and thumb to grasp objects)
•Transfers objects between hands (beginning of crossing midline skills)
•Grabs crayons with a fisted grasp
•Can hold two small objects in one hand
•Begins to show a preference for one hand over the other (beginning development of right handed vs. left handed)

## 12-18 months old

•Can build a tower of 2 blocks high
•Claps hands together (beginning of bilateral coordination)
•Waves goodbye
•Can scoop objects with a spoon or small shovel
•Bangs objects together using both hands (beginning of bilateral coordination)
•Puts small objects into a container
•Scribbles with crayons on paper

## 18 Months – 2 years old

•Putting rings on pegs
•Begins holding a crayon with finger tips and thumb
•Removing pegs from a pegboard
•Marks or scribbles with a crayon or pencil
•Can build a tower 3-4 blocks high
•Can open loosely wrapped packages or containers
•Begins to start cutting paper with scissors (closer to 2 years old)
•Can turn pages in a book one page at a time

## 2 Years old

•Manipulates clay or play dough
•Can stack a block tower 9 blocks high
•Can turn doorknobs
•Can pick up small objects with pincer grasp (index finger and thumb)
•Can complete 3 piece puzzles
•Scribbles
•Make snips on paper with scissors
•Will wash hands independently
•Can screw lids on containers on and off
•Can string large beads

•Zips and unzips large zippers

•Can use a spoon correctly

## 3 Years Old

•Can draw a circle after being shown model

•Cuts a piece of paper in half

•Copies prewriting lines of vertical, horizontal, and circle shapes

•Laces a card

•Can unbutton large buttons

•Can cut a long a wide line with 1/2″ accuracy

•Will string 1/2 inch beads

•Cuts along a line with no more than 1/8-1/4 inch deviation from the l inch

•Sorts objects

•Will fasten and unfasten large buttons

Once you understand the developmental sequence of fine motor skills, it is easy to know what to expect from your child! Fine motor skills are really part of every day life! Here are just a few examples of day-to-day activities that require fine motor skills:

•Getting dressed (manipulating buttons, zippers, and snaps)

•Eating (holding a fork, spoon, or butter knife)

•Fixing meals & snacks (opening or twisting lids & containers, spreading items with a butter knife)

These are just a few ideas! These are tons of ways to include fine motor practice and skills into your daily routine! And what is great is that many of these items are just things you probably already have lying around the house! Here are a few ideas:

- Tongs
- Tweezers
- Cotton Balls
- Beads (large enough to not pose a choking hazard)
- Play dough
- Finger Paint (doubles as a great sensory activity too!)
- Dried pasta
- Lacing cards
- Blocks
- Musical instruments
- Books

**For more from Heather, check out:**
http://goldenreflectionsblog.com/

# Creative Movement

## BY ASHLEY FRATELLO OF ONE MINDFUL MOM

Every human being has an innate desire to move. It emits a sense of pride and fulfillment, starting from those first baby steps to that big 5K marathon.

Movement is a joyful stage of a child's development. Gross motor skills, such as walking, running, jumping, crawling, throwing and dancing, are all key parts of not only body awareness, exercise and growth, but every day play as well.

By the time a child reaches the age of 5 years old, s/he has been introduced to a variety of gross motor skills. Learning these abilities through playful games & independent exploration is a great way to encourage the process of absorbing physical skills essential for the present and future.

## Follow Me!

Take note of your child's favorite moves. Does s/he like to hop? Stomp? Does s/he like to tip-toe? Now think of the moves that are not-so-easy. Is a slow walk difficult for her? What about climbing steps? Use "Follow Me!" as a way to support all skills, increase vocabulary, and work on observation abilities.

> •"Hannah! Look at Daddy – he is hopping over the sidewalk cracks. Follow me while we do it, too! Hop, hop, hop."
> •"Jimmy, I know those steps look kind of tricky. Follow me! Hold my hand and we will climb them together – climb, climb, climb."

Adding an action word to the movement, such as *hop* and *climb*, keeps a rhythm and matches words to your little one.

Consider adding a song to your game, such as this one, set to the tune of *Row, Row, Row Your Boat:*

> Climb, climb, climb away,
> Follow me this way!
> You can do it; so can I.
> We will climb all day!

## Obstacle Course

Challenging your toddler's gross motor skills with "Obstacle Course" is a good way to practice, refine and have a little fun. You can create an obstacle course using a variety of materials and ideas. All you need is a safe, open space and a little imagination.

Here are some ideas for this activity, using simple household objects. Create stations in a backyard, or set them up in a row for your toddler to plough through alongside Mom and Dad.

- •Use a hoolah hoop to teach hopping, spatial awareness and counting. Place it on the floor and encourage your child to hop in and out three times.
- •Toss a beanbag into a bucket. Show your toddler how to toss overhand and underhand. This is also a good way to see which side they favor (left or right).
- •Kick a ball into an overturned garbage can.
- •Toss a beach ball to your child to work on catching. You might notice they clap, turn their head or put their hands to their chest while attempting to catch.

•Walk along a line slowly, quickly or sideways. This will help with balance, too!

•Set up an empty box with the bottom and top open to make a tunnel. Show your child how to crawl through it. Surprise them on the other side by saying "boo!"

•Help your toddler climb over a step-stool by holding their hand.

As s/he grows older, you will notice that her skills will become more refined and s/he will discover different ways to approach each challenge. Keep these materials handy, or switch them up to make your obstacle course fresh and exciting!

**Dance With Me**

The simplest way to encourage your child to use gross motor skills is to play music and dance around the room. Any action can be done to the beat of the music – that is how a dance is formed! Creative movement is a great way to continue the development of gross motor skills, as well as expand the imagination, introduce music appreciation and dramatic play.

Select one movement and repeat it while saying the action in a sing-song voice. Stop the music and freeze. Pick another movement and continue with the pattern of "stop" and "go". Get silly by lowering the volume and matching your body to the softness of the sound, like crawling or walking on tip-toes. Then turn the music up, expand your movements, and get wild and crazy!

You can also add props to make the dances more creative. Party streamers are great for non-locomotor movements, such as swaying, bending knees, waving, marching in place and spinning. These moves are just as important as locomotor skills -- They get the body grooving, but don't necessarily travel across the space.

**For more from Ashley, visit:**
http://onemindfulmom.com/

# Reading Activities for Early Comprehension

### BY KIM VIJ OF
### THE EDUCATORS' SPIN ON IT

Books are one of the most important elements of your Tot School program for your child. Comprehension is a process that occurs before, during, and after your child reads a book. Vocabulary development and comprehension plays an important role in building these skills with your child. How do we start to build steps for success for our children? Here are a few ways to get started laying a foundation for success for your child.

## Make Books Readily Available

It's best throughout the day, to find ways to incorporate a variety of ways to read stories with your child. During your morning routine, breakfast, bath time, bedtime, afternoon break, car ride, and more, there are so many ways to include in books in a child's day. Have a few locations throughout your home to contain your books in order to build a print rich environment for your child. Book baskets, a child sized bookshelf, or even a special library book bag will become treasured spots for you and your child to enjoy story time. If your child is a little rough with books there are so many available in board book format. Teaching proper book care is an important step too.

## Reading with a Plan

One element to consider is adding books with a theme to focus on concepts you're learning in other areas. Some common literacy themes include animals, transportation, insects, dinosaurs, school, pumpkins, fall, winter, spring, classic stories, etc.. Check out your local library's reservation system; many times you can search online and reserve books to avoid having to spend time searching at the library.

## Finding Story Elements Together

Once you've selected a focused theme or book, creating reading activities becomes easy. As you select a specific book take a look at the specific elements of the story. You can focus on the main character, setting, and story elements to create an activity for your child to complete. By focusing on these elements you're encouraging your child to begin to learn how to focus on story comprehension. As you're reading a story pause and ask questions about what's happening. It starts out with simple pointing to parts in the pictures on the book and becomes verbal responses to your questions. As your child enters school, they will even start to have to write out the details they recall from a story. It's so important to begin to build the basic steps at home to prepare them for success in school. Creating a story together of a shared experience can be a way to help build a child's understanding of how books work. Plus, it can become their first chance to be able to "read a story" all by themselves. A recent trip to a park, visit from a friend, or even a recent event makes the best content.

## Making Story Time Hands On

As you read the story, think of materials around your house that you can use for retelling the story. You'd be surprised at the toys you have that relate in some way to a story. Expect for your child to ask you to read a story over and over again; they are learning rhymes and language development as you're doing that, so keep it up! Some of us may be challenged with reading to active toddlers, with a few creative moments you'll discover what works best for them. They need story time just as much as others so keep at it, eventually they will discover the magic of books! Finding a character they love, animal or even a funny character voices might be the secret to get them started.

Creating Sensory Bins based on stories can provide hours of hands on activities. Find a few elements from the story and place them into a box. Consider adding a few word cards or letters that tie into the story in some way. For example, if you're reading The Very Hungry Caterpillar, you might consider adding the words egg, chrysalis, caterpillar, eat, and butterfly or even the days of the week. Plus you could add pictures or the actual objects from the story along with an item that they can sort through for sensory and vocabulary development. Creating a story basket or story box with items that relate to the story will help your child build comprehension skills along with skills of the activities that are based in literacy, math, science, or the arts.

## Creative Movement with Stories

Once you've selected a book, it can be a lot of fun to create activities that go with the book. Think of ways to recreate the character, puppets, paper plates, or art projects can be a playful way to recreate the main characters. Encourage your child to retell the story using their new creation. Finding ways to create movement with the story will make it a playful experience for your child, and often times even more memorable. Think of ways to get them involved. Can they...

Run like the Gingerbread Man?
Crawl or eat like the Hungry Caterpillar?
Drive a pretend bus like the Pigeon?
Wear a striped hat like Cat in the Hat?
Share their rainbow scales like a fish?

## Building Literacy Success in your Home

Surrounding your child with books during Tot School and providing them with opportunities to experience books in their environment will help to create solid foundation for their love of books. Creating ways to discuss books and their story elements will help your child learn the skills needed for story comprehension as they begin to learn to read. It all starts with having books readily available in our homes!

**For more from Kim, check out:**
http://www.theeducatorsspinonit.com/

# Using 3-Part cards to Build Vocabulary

## BY DANIELLE SHABER OF
## BLESSEDLY BUSY

Toddlers are naturally curious. They are interested in all of the things around them. It is our job to expand their world and give them the words to talk about it. Vocabulary is one of the most important things that you can teach your toddler.

One way to increase a toddlers' vocabulary is to use 3-part cards. These little cards are particularly helpful if you don't have/can't find the item you want to teach your child. They are also very portable, which makes visits to the doctor a little easier.

A set of 3-part cards have been included in this book. For this example, I will show you how to use them to teach a toddler about shapes as a part of early math. However, these ideas will work for any 3-part cards that you have and for any subject.

**Find Out What They Know**
Do you know how many shapes your toddler can name? I sure didn't! I had a rough idea, but it wasn't until I put the cards in front of her that I knew for sure.

**Introducing the New Shapes**
Decide what shapes you want to focus on. You want the activity to be interesting without being overwhelming. Don't worry if you don't pick the right amount at first, you can always add or take away cards. I chose to start with four shapes. I chose four that are very different from each other and ones that she seemed to recognize but not always know the name for.

74

## Step 1

Using either set of cards (no labels or labels) put one of them on the table in front of your toddler. Have the following conversation—or something like it.
> "This is a heart. Trace the heart with your finger and say heart."
> "Heart."
> "Good job! Let's do another one."

Continue until you feel like they know them or are done working for the day.

## Step 2

Put the cards in front of your toddler.
> "Can you find the triangle?"

If they struggle: quit for today and pick up on step 1 tomorrow. Let them know they worked really hard today! If they knew all of the shapes, move on to step 3.

## Step 3

Show your toddler each card and ask, "What shape is this?" If they struggle: quit for today and pick up on step 1 tomorrow. Let them know they worked really hard today! If they knew all of the shapes, move on to step 4

## Step 4

Start with the cards that have the words on them spread out in front of your toddler. Make a pile of the other shape cards and the word cards.

Show your toddler how to pick a shape card and match it to the other shape. You might say: "This card is a heart. Hmmm, I wonder where the other heart is. Can you find the other heart? There it is! Let's put the two hearts together."

Once all of the shapes are matched, go through the shapes saying each name.

Now it's time for the word cards. Even though your toddler probably can't read, it's still useful to have them match the word cards. It might look like this: "Look! Here is a word. Let's match it up to the other words to see what it is.

(Place the word under one of the words on the table). Do these look the same? No? How about these, are these the same word? Yes!"

It took my toddler a few tries to understand how to compare the words. It's not as obvious as comparing shapes. Comparing the words challenges your toddler to look carefully and see the differences that are minor in comparison to the picture of the shape.

## If Your Child Struggles

Don't worry. Every child is different and is ready at different times. The real reasons to do any activity with a toddler are to have fun and spend time with you. Learning is a bonus. Here are some things that you can try:

- *Do less*. Either less words or less amount of time. I started with 4 that she already sort of knew. For her, I would probably start with just two new words. If it was my oldest when she was 3, I could have done the whole stack in a day or two. Listen to your toddler and follow their lead.
- *Take a break*. Sometimes we just need some time to process what we are learning. Everyone. Not just toddlers. Give both of you a break and try it again in a few days.
- *Try a different approach*. Below you will find other ways to increase vocabulary with the 3-part cards.

## Variations

It can get kind of boring, for parent and child, to do the same thing each time. I have found changing something small in an activity helpful in bringing it back to life.
Not all of these activities will work with any 3-part card set. This is just to give you some ideas to get started.

## Add Movement

- Have your child use a fly swatter to swat the correct card that you call out. My son especially loves this one!
- Set the stacks in different parts of the room so that the child has to leave to go get the next card. Perfect for working off energy & improving concentration.

•Create an obstacle course out of furniture with the stacks of cards on opposite sides of the room.

## Add Sensory
•Put cards in a bin of rice and have your toddler find all of the cards to match.
•Trace the shape with glue:  adds interest when your toddler traces the shape and says its name.
•Use play dough or pipe cleaners to create the shapes while talking about them.

## Change How They Are Presented
Print both pages, but only cut out the page with the words & the picture separate.  On the back of each word & picture you can attach a magnet or Velcro.  Now your toddler can match them on top of the sheet you didn't cut apart.  Not only does it make it easier for your toddler, you now have an activity that travels easy.  (If you use magnets, take a cookie sheet from the dollar store.  They are the perfect size for a sheet of paper.)

## Games & Extensions
- Memory (Need 2 sets)
- Go fish (Need 2 sets)
- Find one physical object per card and have your toddler match it with the vocabulary card
- Use the cards as titles and have your child sort a lot of objects
- Go on a scavenger hunt.  See how many shapes you can find.

•Play "I-Spy" with whatever is around you.  Great for when your toddler needs a distraction.

*Find our 3 part cards in the appendix.*

**For more from Danielle, visit:**
http://blessedlybusy.com/

# Printable Activities *for* Toddlers

## BY VIVIANA OF TOTSCHOOLING

## Why Printables?

When my first daughter was a toddler, she loved those wooden puzzles where you match the puzzle pieces to the pictures. I bought a lot of those puzzles and had quite a collection. However, storage became a bit of a problem. Also, often times I would think of a subject I wanted my daughter to learn and I wouldn't be able to find a puzzle for it. Eventually I came to realize that I could design my own matching activities that can be printed, laminated and used in a very similar way as those puzzles. My daughter loved my printables and has learned a lot from them over the years.

Here are some benefits of printables for toddlers:
- great tool for teaching or reinforcing many different concepts
- builds vocabulary, visual discrimination, and fine motor skills
- very portable and can be taken anywhere for a quick and convenient activity
- encourages quiet, independent work in older toddlers
- unique & fun learning activity that kids love

In the following pages, you will find a set of toddler printables that I created especially for this eBook. These printables will help your child learn and build vocabulary about various subjects, such as animals, body parts, foods, emotions, vehicles and household objects. Follow the directions below for how to prepare and use the printables.

## How to Use Printables

Typically, printable activities can be used with toddlers 18 months and up, or whenever the child's visual and fine motor skills are developed enough to be able to match pictures. The printables should be laminated for durability, and I always recommend that you use velcro for all the loose pieces. This keeps the pieces from shifting out of place and will prevent your toddler from getting frustrated. After preparing the printables, you will have a set of activities that your toddler can do over and over again, and that you can use with future children.

**Here are the materials needed:**
- color printer
- laminator
- pack of laminating pouches
- pack of clear velcro

Each printable activity consists of 2 pages. The first page becomes the laminated activity mat, and the second page gets cut to create the puzzle pieces for your child to match to the activity mat.

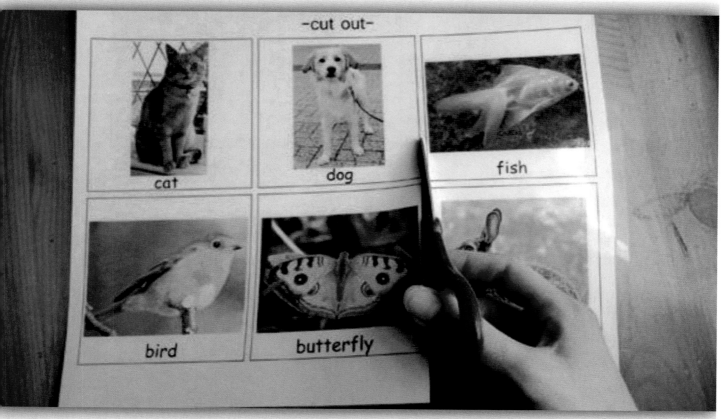

**Step 1**: Laminate all pages.

**Step 2**: Cut out the squares on the 2nd page of each activity, labeled with the words "-cut out-" at the top. If sharp corners are a concern, you can cut off the tips of each square.

**Step 3:** Attach a small piece of transparent velcro to the middle of each picture on the activity mat, and also to the back of each puzzle piece.

I hope your child loves these printables! You can find printable activities at the end of this book and even more printables for toddlers and preschoolers on my blog.

**For more from Viviana, check out:**
http://www.totschooling.net/

# *10-15 Months*
## BY ALECIA FRANCOIS OF
## LEARNING 2 WALK

Wow, can you believe it? Your baby is no longer a baby. If you are lucky, those lovely late night feeds have ended and you may be getting more than five hours of sleep per night. If not, no worries, just remember to make a note of all these late night sessions for when your baby becomes a teenager.

Your little one is now going through numerous changes and at a rapid rate, especially between 10 and 15 months. "What changes?" you may ask and "What can I do to further help my little one?" Here is a snapshot of what is going on with your tiny tot as well as activities you can do to help them in their development.

## Development of a 10-15 Month Old

So your tot is growing by leaps and bounds. Here are a few things you can expect at this stage.

- Crawls and/or attempts to walk
- The ability to say 2 or 3 words
- Holds on to furniture and toddles
- Takes things out of containers
- Picks up small items off the floor
- Looks at a person who is saying their name

# Activities You Can Do With Your 10-15 Month Old

*Please note these activities are to be done with parental guidance.*

### What's That Sound? (Auditory Development)

- Needed: cellphone alarm (or any alarm) ; 2 or 3 objects that can hide the alarm
- Place the 2 or 3 objects in different areas of the room and set the alarm to go off. See if your tot can identify where the alarm is coming from. If your tot figures it out right away, simply add more hiding places and enjoy.

### Tearing Paper (Fine Motor Skills)

- Needed: loose paper, old magazines
- If you have loose paper or magazines sitting on your shelf that are no longer being used, put your tot's fingers to use. Simply give your tot a sheet of paper and demonstrate what needs to be done. Tear the piece of paper any way you like. Overemphasize what you are doing and make funny faces if you must. Your tot will get a kick out of it and you will enjoy it too.
- Once you are finished with demonstrating, hand a sheet of paper to your tot to see how they handle it. I have found that larger sheets work best for beginners.

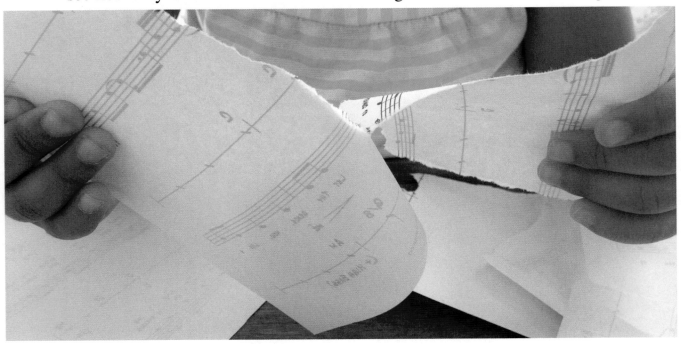

### Bombs Away (Fine Motor Skills)

- Needed: Cheerios, 2 bowls
- Pour a few Cheerios (or any small hard food object) into the first bowl. Demonstrate a few times how to pick up one Cheerio from one bowl and drop it in the other . Allow your tot to do the same.

*Unwrap the Toy (Fine a Motor Skills)*

Needed: tissue paper, small toy

Wrap a small toy belonging to your tot in layers of tissue paper. Allow your tot to undo the tissue paper in order to find their toy.

*Walk the Box (Gross Motor Skills)*

Needed: A cardboard box of similar height to your tot

The aim of this activity is to allow your tot to walk while pushing the box. This is especially great if your tot is currently toddling from one piece of furniture to the other but has not let go yet. Ensure that the box you choose is not too light or too heavy. It needs to be sturdy enough that it moves with your tot.

These are just a few of the activities that I have planned for my 10 month old. There are tons more on Pinterest or on the internet. Simply search for "activities for 10-15 month old". To see my son's schedule for the next few months as well as a blank planning sheet, see appendix. His schedule is simply a list of activities that I keep on the fridge so that I can get a quick glance of what I can do with him for the day. I aim to do 2 activities every week, placing a checkmark on the sheet each day I do the activity.

Remember to enjoy your young one at this stage and don't forget that every tot moves at their own pace.

*Find our planning schedule in the appendix.*

**For more from Alecia, check out:**
http://learning2walk.com/

# 15-18 Months: Exploration
## BY VANESSA THIEL OF
## MAMA'S HAPPY HIVE

Fifteen to eighteen months of age is a wonderful time of exploration of our amazing world through play. Children love to wander around and check out everything in their sphere, however, they still need the comfort of knowing their parent is close by. The toddler at this age is learning language development, outdoor play, social play, and everyday life skills for both fine and gross motor development. For language development, it is important to give everything a name in the child's environment and also to read to your child everyday. I am going to share several activities that my little one has enjoyed at this age.

**Transfer Activities – Helpful (dog food, dustpan, laundry, diaper), Ball, Shapes**
This is also a great age to start teaching your child to be helpful around the home. Once the toddler learns to walk, they love to transfer objects from one spot to the next. Toddlers have fun carrying a ball outside on the grass, while practicing walking/running between mom and dad. They also enjoy carrying laundry to the hamper, transferring dirt in a dustpan to the trashcan, and transporting the dog food for the dog's dish.

**Sensory Activities**
This is a delightful age to immerse your child in sensory activities that involve all five senses. A wonderful sense to develop is the sense of touch with various textured fabrics, objects hidden in a rice bowl, water play, and anything that you can dream up. I put a sensory bin full of rose petals in water for my little boy to enjoy as well as a fun tub of cooked spaghetti for him to sit in. Both activities were a big hit for my little one.

## Opposites: Open/Close, Inside/Outside, On/Off

This age is a wonderful time to teach children the meaning & words for opposites. This can be done by saying the word "open" as you open the door and "close" as you close the door. The same can be done for "on" & "off" of a light switch or the blender. We learned about the concept of "inside" and "outside" by flower arranging. My little boy loved to place the flowers "inside" the vase and then take them out again.

## For more from Vanessa, check out:
http://www.mamashappyhive.com/

# 18-24 Months: Play
## BY LINDSAY EIDAHL OF
## MY CREATIVE DAYS

Planning activities for toddlers is so much fun! Toddlers are curious and love exploring the world that surrounds them so much that every little activity becomes a learning experience for them. Activities for toddlers do not have to be extravagant. The simplest things seem to resonate the most with toddlers.

Some of my favorite activities with toddlers are those that encourage spontaneous play. It is introducing something to the toddler and seeing how he/she plays with it without prompting. Introducing pots and pans with some wooden spoons is an afternoon full of excitement and musical madness. A set of blocks can be a great activity for toddlers. Not only can they stack them and knock them over, but they can line them up, count them, and name their colors. Try setting out some of the things you may have in your recycling bin; milk lids, soup cans and toilet paper rolls and see how many different things the toddler can come up with.

Another way you can introduce spontaneous play is through sensory bins. Sensory bins are full of different materials that the kids can feel, manipulate, count and play with how he/she sees fit. A sensory can be big or small. It can have lots of things in it or just a few. It is fun to come up with different "themed" sensory bins.

For instance, create sensory bins based on the season like a fall sensory bin. Of course, it is also fun to introduce a toddler to a structured, planned out activity as well. This is great for teaching them how to follow directions, be creative and start and complete a task. Some of my favorite "structured activities" for toddlers are on the next page.

86

## Counting Pom-Poms on Popsicle Sticks

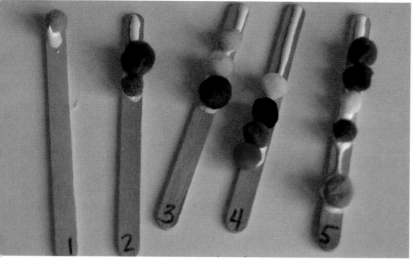

Playing can be found in anything at any time and any place. It's about being creative to find the learning opportunity for your child!

## Build a Recycled Snowman

**For more from Lindsay check out:**
http://www.mycreativedays.com/

# 24-36 Months: Science
### BY MONIQUE B OF
## LIVING LIFE & LEARNING

Science is about discovery and encouraging children to explore the world around them. Children will find a lot of joy while they take a look at the birds around them , rocks from the playground and webs in the corner of your house. Yes, I'm not as proficient at eliminating all of them.

I love getting into those fun messy projects because those are what I believe my children will remember the most. Do you talk about which colors make green or is it better to show them? They get to experience what you mean through hands on activities. At this age, toddlers and preschoolers are full of questions and this is a great time to introduce new science vocabulary and get them excited by the world around them.

The best way to start learning about science is to go on nature walks and discuss what you see, why you are seeing those things? Are seasons changing, is that a habitat or home for someone, or how did that flower get there? Ask questions and answer your child's questions as well. By doing this you invite them to ask questions for themselves.

## Fun Foaming Flour
- large bowl
- mixing cups or spoons
- 4 cups of flour
- 1/4 cup of baking soda
- food coloring
- water
- vinegar

Mix the flour and baking soda in a large bowl. Add water or vinegar in each of the cups or spoons and add food coloring to each. I had my child add two spoons of colored water before she added a spoonful of vinegar and it was great to see her reaction because she was not expecting it.

My daughter started to blow the "bubbles" that started to foam. We had a wooden spoon to mix the 'dough' to mix and I thought that she would use her hands to explore but she doesn't like to get messy so it was contained in the bowl. You could definitely get your hands in there and form a dough but my kids like to keep adding liquids so it turned into a soup mixture that they enjoyed mixing with a wooden spoon as they watched the colors change.

## Water absorption

- coffee filters
- non-permanent markers
- glass cups
- water

Fill the glass cups with 1-2 cm of water. Color your filters with concentric circles starting from the middle of the filter. Leave some spacing so that you can see how the water moves before it blends with the next color. Fold the filter in half 3 times until you end up with a triangle and then place it into the cup, pointy side down. Wait for several minutes and watch. Use different colors to get various effects. Talk about how the colors change as the run into another one. Talk about the direction of the water movement as well.

## Toilet Paper Roll Course

- paper towel rolls
- toilet paper rolls
- tape
- different sized balls
- blocks

- toys
- cars and trucks

Cut the rolls in half and the tape the together to form long tracks. You will need to lay them on a ramp, I used the lid from a toy box. Get different toys or objects and race them down the tracks. Talk about why one would go further than another. What characteristics they need to have to roll down the tracks. What material is it made from? The weight or size of the object and how that would influence its speed. This is always a fun game with my older boys as well.

## Magnet fun
- magnet attached to string and pole
- objects made of different materials: balls, wooden or plastic blocks, metal lids, buttons, toy cars

Go fishing for different objects and discuss the characteristics of the objects that the magnet stick to. What makes it attracted to the magnet? See what other objects around the home the magnet sticks to like the fridge or stove.

**For more from Monique, check out:**
http://www.livinglifeandlearning.com/

# How to Transition to Preschool or Homeschool

## BY KIM VIJ OF

## THE EDUCATORS' SPIN ON IT

Preparing children for school with Tot School is one of most important things that you can do for your child to insure success as they enter more formal education. For some it might be entering Preschool or for others it may be Kindergarten when they first enter a formal class setting. By using a few simple tools and strategies, your child will be ready to start this new journey of school.

## Exposure to Group Settings

One key element to include in your Tot School is to create opportunities for your child to learn and be in a group setting with one adult giving directions. You can do this in a variety of ways. To create group settings with Tot School, it's recommended to take turns hosting the content of the lesson each week with a variety of parent leaders. This gives your child the opportunity to follow directions from an adult other than you. Taking turns reading the story, leading in songs, or giving directions for a game or craft are all roles that your child will learn to listen carefully and receive directions from an adult. Participating in a local library's program, music and/or dance classes, religious, education, or athletic programs can provide practice in following other adult leaders too.

## Read Books About School

Providing opportunities for your child to read books about school will introduce them to the concept of a classroom and the classroom structure. There are some great series that are based in a school setting both in books as well as television shows that make it easier to explore the concept of formal education. Purposefully exposing your child to these opportunities is ideal, planning to discuss with them about school afterwards is also important.

## Learn about the Elements of School

When helping your child prepare for enrolling for school, discussions can make a big difference in their feelings towards starting. Helping your child learn to identify what the setting will be like, opportunities they will have, and the schedule of it all can help with this new routine in their life. As you begin to consider school enrollment and start to narrow down your options, it's recommended to take your child with you to the school for a tour. Allow them to observe the settings and materials available; afterwards, talk about how they felt while they were there. If you're homeschooling, finding a local Homeschool Co-op to participate in can be helpful. Finding the right setting for your child in a school can be stressful so give yourself time and be prepared. Creating a book with your child about school can be one way to build confidence and ease anxieties about this new transition. Take time to read this book together the weeks before school start; it helps give them a little control of the new things to come.

## Celebrate the First Day of School

Create ways to celebrate the first day of school with your child. Magic Dust for the night before, countdown chain, or a calendar are ways to mark this special occasion. Getting a child involved in packing their school lunch or going supply shopping can make the occasion special. Be prepared for how you want to create your child's first day of school photo; it's a treasured keepsake. For public or private school, attending events like meet the teacher & open house can help parents know the expectations & guidelines that your child's school will have. The most important part is to start the routine of school before school starts to help adjust with the early mornings and bedtime routines.

Having a plan for starting school help make this transition successful for your child and for you.

**For more from Kim, check out:**
http://www.theeducatorsspinonit.com

# About the Authors

## Kara Carrero

Kara is a former classroom teacher turned homeschooler, curriculum writer, and web consultant. Her passion has always been in education and to tot-school is an extension of that love. She blogs at ALLterNATIVElearning and can be found on Facebook, Pinterest, and Instagram.

## Erin Buhr

Erin is an Early Childhood specialist, freelance writer, & mama of twins. She lives with her husband and three year olds in Mississippi where she enjoys traveling, taking photos, & being outside in the sun. She has a Master's Degree in ECE & was an Early Childhood Educator for 11 years before deciding to stay home with her own children. She blogs at Bambini Travel, hoping to inspire exploration & travel with young children.

## Katie T. Christiansen

Katie has worked as an early childhood professional for 13 years and has a degree in Early Childhood Education. She currently owns and operates her own private preschool and shares some of her perspectives, activities, and adventures at Preschool Inspirations.

## Jennifer Tammy

Jennifer is a single mom dedicated to pursuing higher education for herself and providing Montessori and Reggio home education to her daughter — and the wonderful children who now join them every weekday to learn, share, explore, & discover as a part of Child's Garden Montessori. Follow on facbook & pinterest.

# Monica Pruett

Monica is an author & blogger at HappyandBlessedHome, where she provides free printables as well as free games and ideas for teaching your toddlers and preschoolers, encouraging words for moms, as well as great ideas for ways to have fun together as a family. Facebook, Google+, Pinterest, Twitter, and Bloglovin'.

Becky Marie is a wife & SAHM to 3 boys living in Central New York State. Their days are filled with race cars, trains, & super heroes. The boys learn through every day activities & play in a Montessori-inspired environment. When the weather is nice you'll find the whole family hiking in the nearby mountains. After discovering a dairy allergy in her second son, Becky has developed a passion for dairy free nutrition & cooking. She blogs about their Montessori Homeschool & Modern Homemaking at ForThisSeason.com.

# Amanda Boyarshinov

Amanda Boyarshinov is one of the bloggers behind the site: The Educators' Spin On It. She has a Master's Degree in Reading Education for grades K-12 and a B.A. in Elementary Education. She shares her teaching knowledge with moms everywhere through her creative, inventive blog posts. She has three kids: ages 1, 4, and 7. Find her on Facebook, Google+, Instagram, Pinterest, and Twitter.

# Emma Edwards

During a difficult pregnancy suffering from Hyperemesis Gravidarum (HG) Emma vowed to make every day an adventure once she had recovered. Adventures of Adam is the outcome of completing a 100 day play challenge with her toddler as part of that promise. Emma has a section dedicated to HG friendly play activities so that Mums can still be part of their children's play whilst they are ill.

# Monique B

Monique is a homeschooling mother to a toddler, 1st and 8th grader. You can find her writing about visual spatial learner, lapbooks, early learning and all the other homeschooling mishaps on Living Life and Learning. She has been homeschooling for 7 years and shares her journey from her imperfect world.

# Danielle Shaber

Danielle is a Middle School Math teacher turned homeschooling mom. She spends her days perfecting organization ideas and creatively teaching her 4 children...especially math! You can read about her progress on her blog Blessedly Busy.

# Birute Efe

Birute Efe has daily fun at her kids activities blog Playtivities and the farm where she lives with her family. She loves creating activities and toys for her 2 kiddos by up-cycling household items, so she will never walk pass by a big cardboard box or a pile of old magazines. She believes the best learning comes from exploring and creating.

# Melissa Misra

Melissa is the creator of swamimommi.com, a blog dedicated to life styling for the job of joyful living! Her focus is on creating resources for kids & families to help reduce stress, increase connection, and make healthy choices. She brings experience in Occupational Therapy, nutrition, & child development, as well as being a mom and wife, to strategies for improving attention and health, and the encouragement of creative play.

# Kimberly Huff

Kimberly is a fun loving homeschool mom to 5. She spends her days helping her children learn, grow, & love the world. She has a background in early childhood education & a passion for raising children up in a positive peaceful way. You can find her writing full time at Natural Beach Living where she shares kids activities, hands on learning, homeschooling, & a love for natural living. Follow her on Facebook, Pinterest, Instagram, and Twitter.

# Heather Gruetman

Heather is a homeschool mom blogger. She worked as an Occupational Therapy Assistant in the public school system before becoming a SAHM to her daughter. She enjoys sharing her tot-school & preschool ideas on GoldenReflectionsBlog.com where she writes about Christian Montessori inspired with an Occupational Therapy twist. You can also find her on Facebook, Pinterest, Twitter, and Google+.

# Ashley Fratello

Ashley Fratello is a writer, educator and theatre performer from Western New York. She has a two year old son and is a strong advocate of learning through play and mindful parenting. Find her at One Mindful Mom.

# Kim Vij

Kim Vij is an early childhood educator and mom of three. She shares her "Educator's Spin" on parenting issues and how to make everyday moments into learning opportunities at The Educators' Spin On It and award winning Pinterest Boards with over 1.5 Million Followers. You can find Kim sharing ideas on Pinterest, Facebook, Twitter, Instagram & Google +.

# Viviana Florea

Viviana is a blogging mom to a toddler and a preschooler, sharing ideas and resources for early learning. With a background in graphic design, she specializes in unique, hands-on printable activities that are educational, fun and inspire creativity in young minds. You can find her printables and learning activities for toddlers and preschoolers on her blog, Totschooling .

# Alecia Francois

Alecia is a pastor's wife, mommy to two and wife to her best friend and trusted sidekick, Mark. She is also a Janadian (Jamaican + Canadian) living in a small town in in Canada. Find her at Learning 2 Walk.

# Vanessa Thiel

Vanessa is a Mama to a very active and adorable toddler named "Little Bee" on her blog, "Mama's Happy Hive," where they are discovering and learning together about the beauty of Montessori education. It has been one of the most delightful journeys she has ever taken and she looks forward to the years of continued discovery with her little one as he grows up.

# Lindsay Eidhal

Lindsay is a mom to Landen and Gabrielle, wife to Matt and blogger at www.mycreativedays.com. She loves to be creative in her day, her home and with her kids. She is obsessed with old wood, rusty treasures and everything in between. Finding frugal and creative ways to decorate the home, create a fabulous craft or do an activity with the kids is one of her passions.

# Appendix

| | | |
|---|---|---|
| Rectangle | Circle | Triangle |
| Square | Rhombus | Oval |
| Heart | Crescent | Trapezoid |

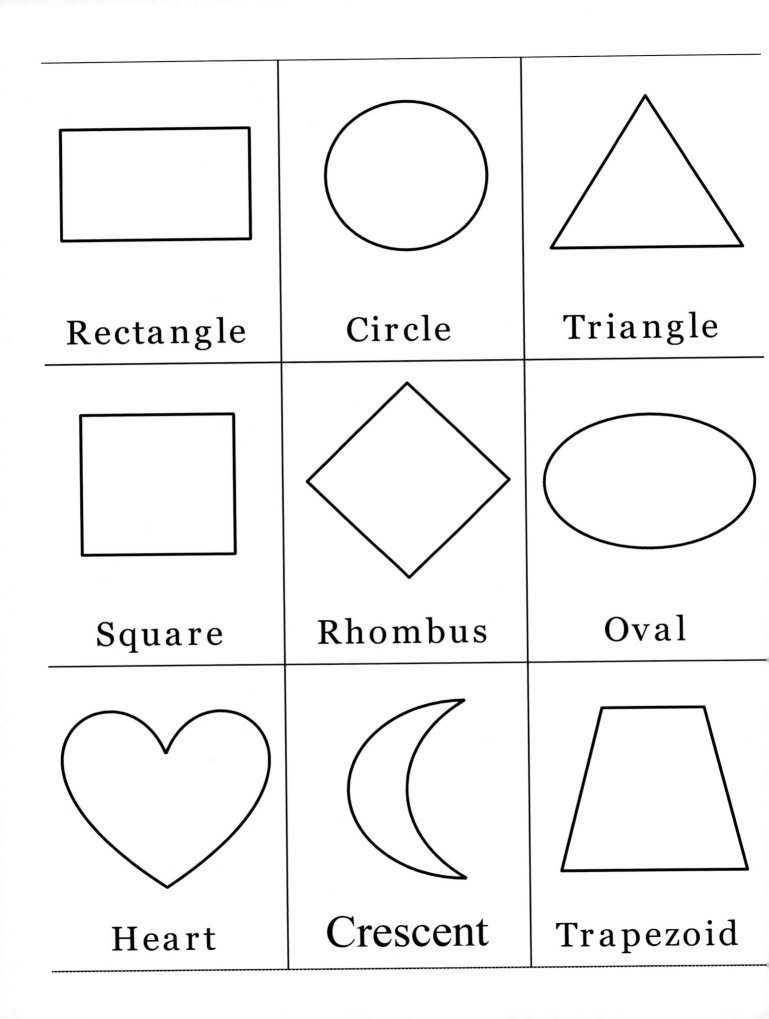

| | | |
|---|---|---|
| Rectangle | Circle | Triangle |
| Square | Rhombus | Oval |
| Heart | Crescent | Trapezoid |

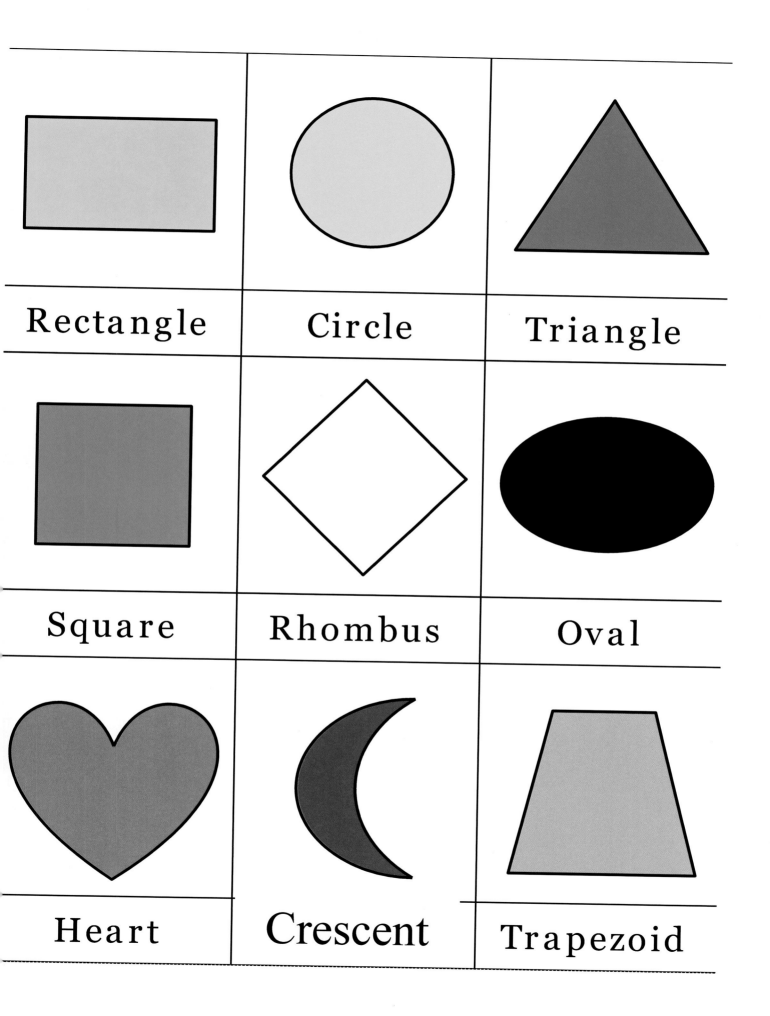

| | | |
|---|---|---|
| Rectangle | Circle | Triangle |
| Square | Rhombus | Oval |
| Heart | Crescent | Trapezoid |

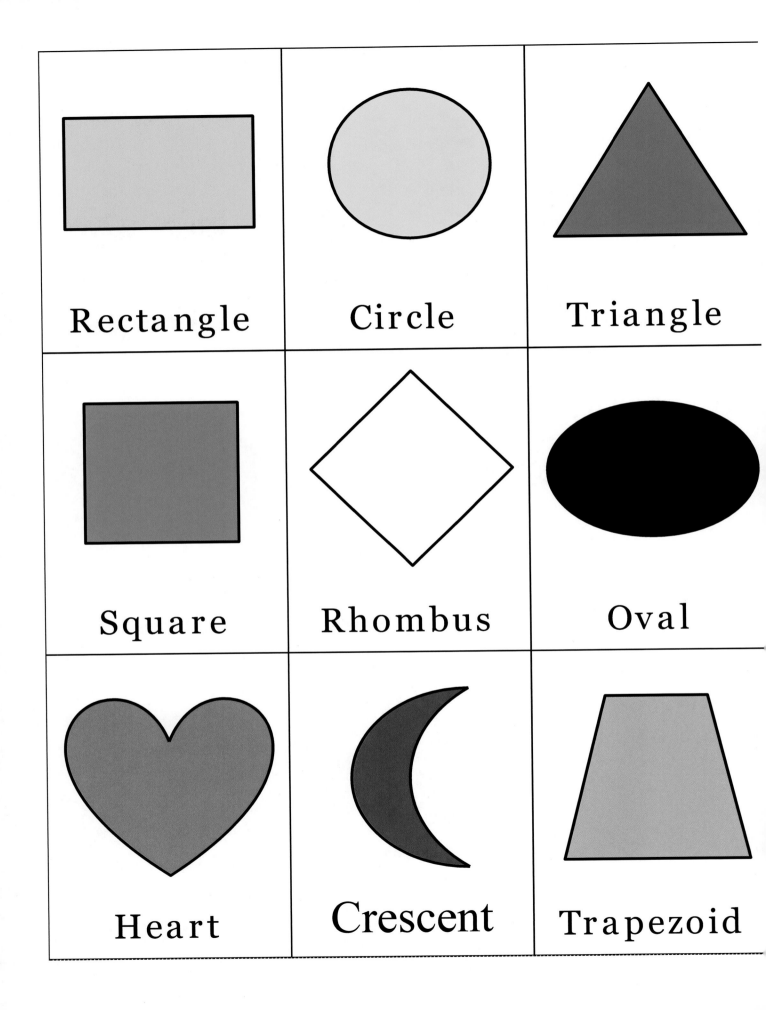

| Rectangle | Circle | Triangle |
| Square | Rhombus | Oval |
| Heart | Crescent | Trapezoid |

**Pets**

bird

cat

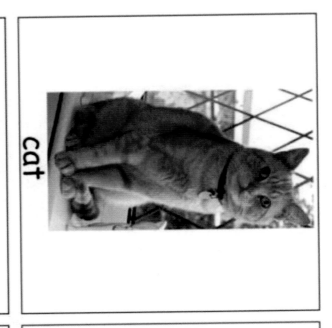

butterfly

dog

-cut out-

rabbit

fish

# Vehicles

bicycle

airplane

truck

train

-cut out-

boat

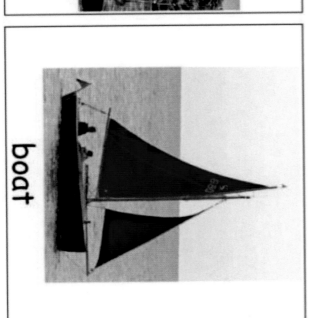

car

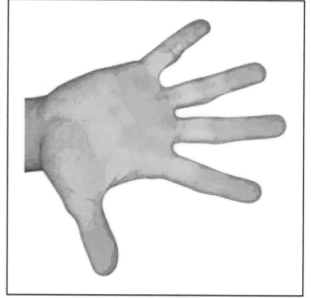

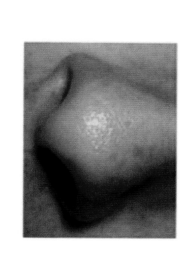

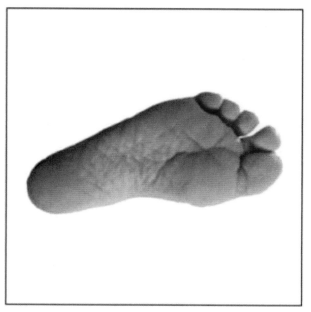

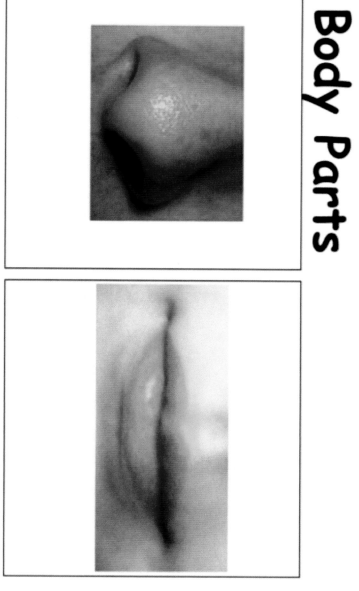

# Body Parts

ear

eyes

hand

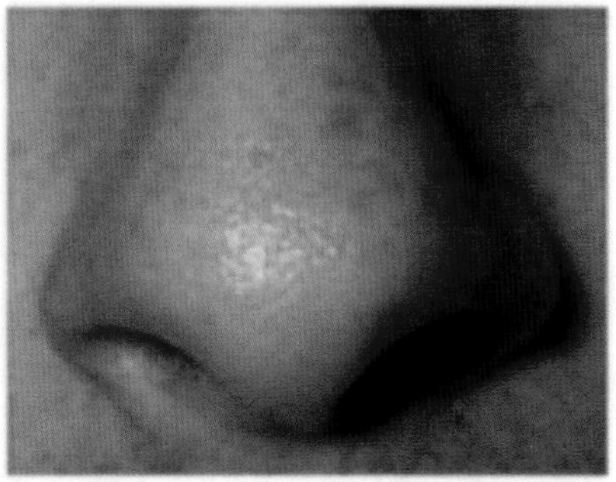

nose

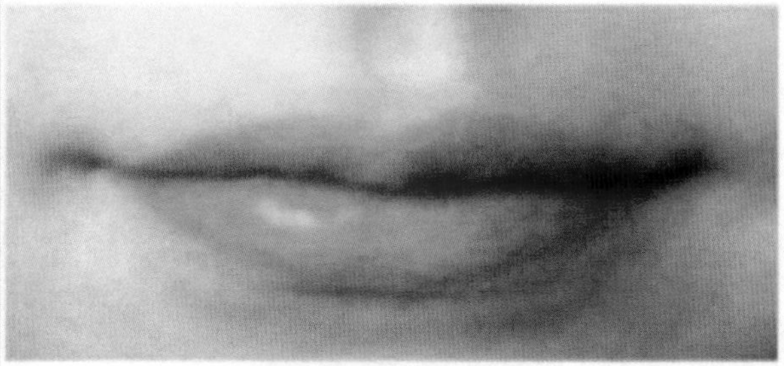

-cut out-

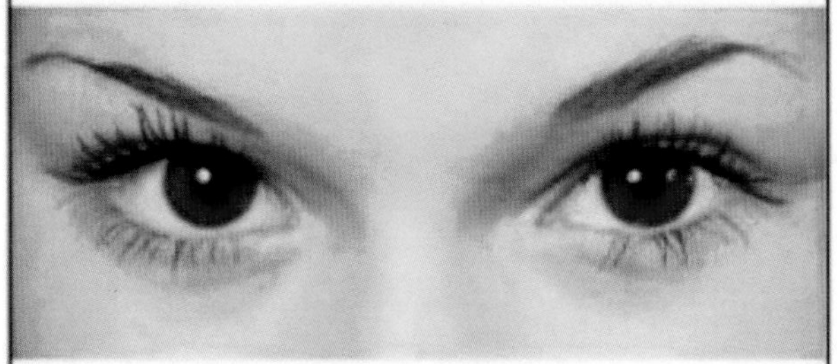

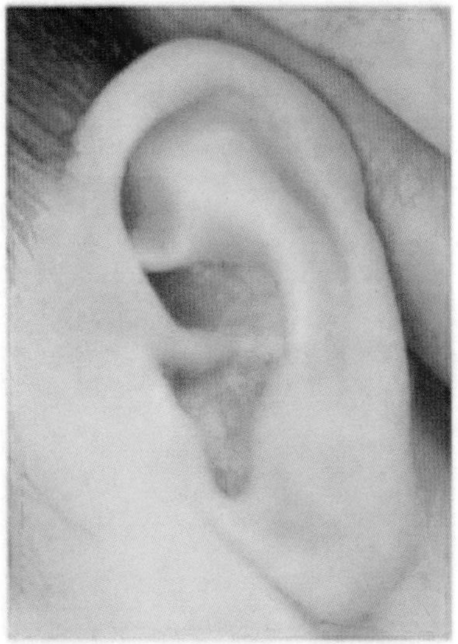

foot

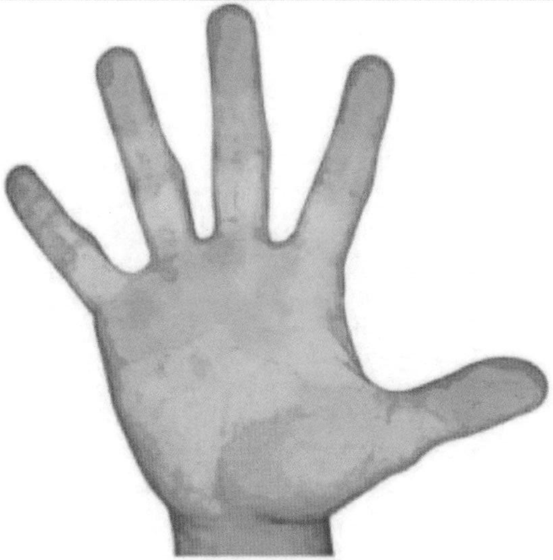

mouth

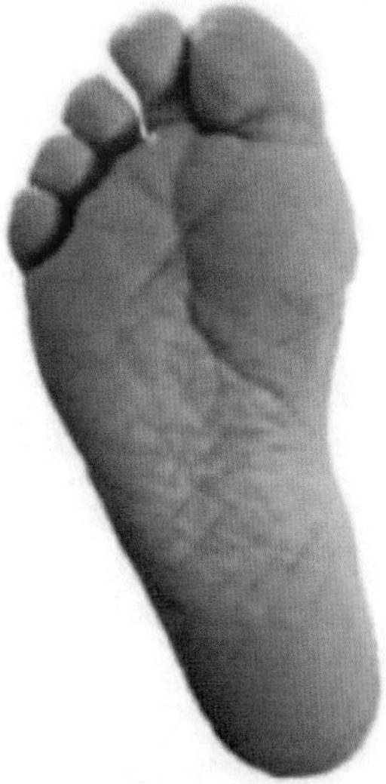

# Farm Animals

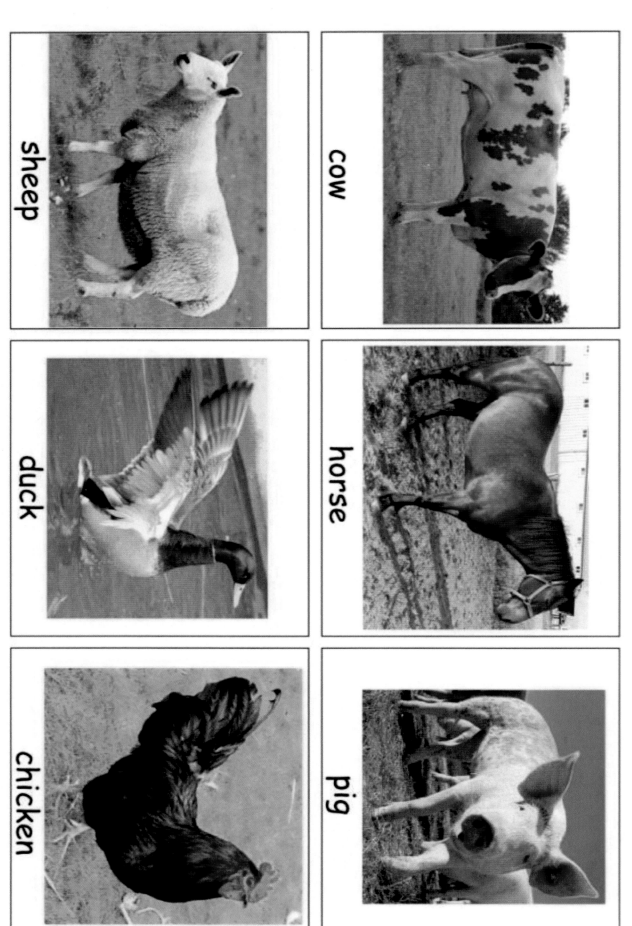

sheep

cow

duck

horse

-cut out-

chicken

pig

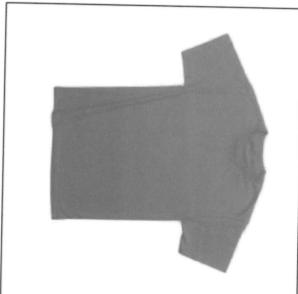

**Clothing**

socks

t-shirt

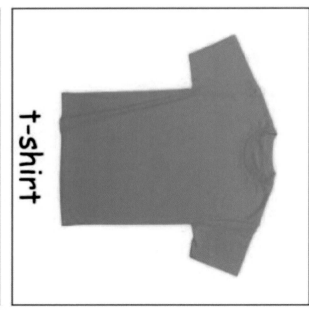

pants

sneakers

-cut out-

jacket

hat

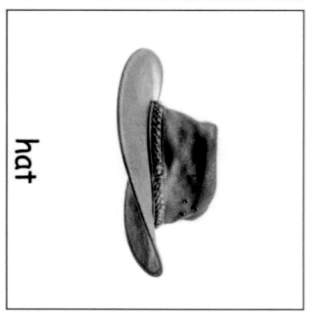

# Emotions

worried

sad

scared

happy

surprised

angry

-cut out-

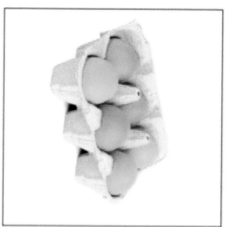

**Foods**

bananas

bread

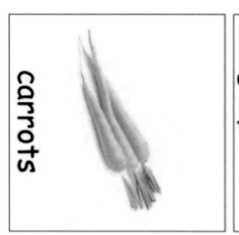

carrots

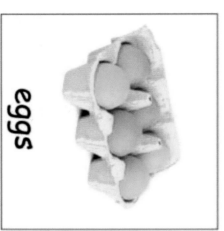

eggs

milk

grapes

strawberry

-cut out-

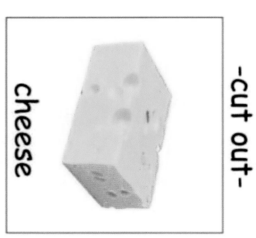

cheese

broccoli

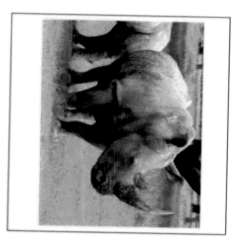

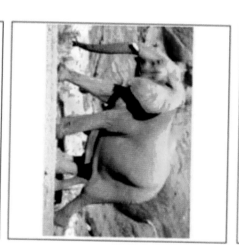

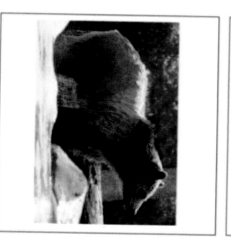

rhinoceros

lion

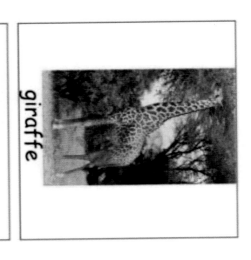

giraffe

-cut out-

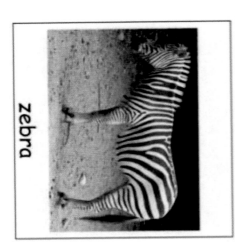

zebra

elephant

hippopotamus

monkey

bear

tiger

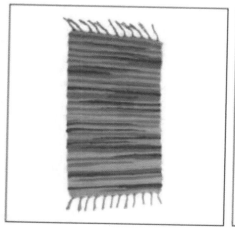

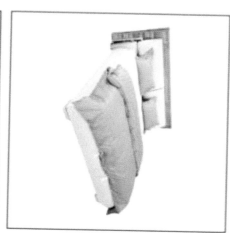

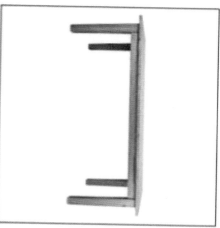

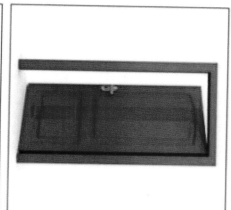

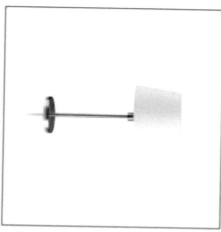

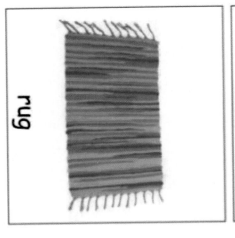

rug

clock

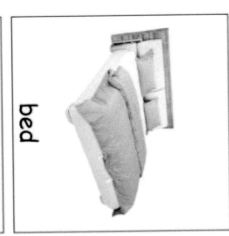

bed

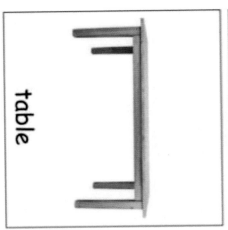

table

door

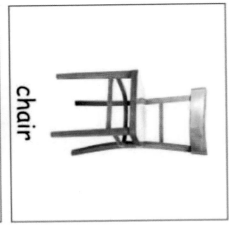

chair

-cut out-

window

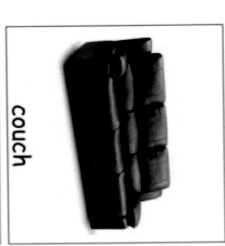

couch

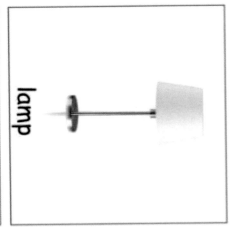

lamp

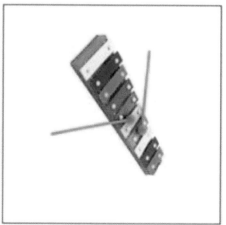

# Musical Instruments

violin

drum

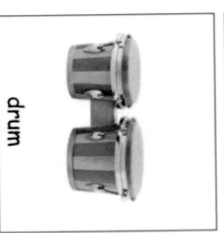

guitar

trumpet

saxophone

flute

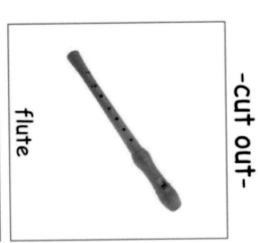

-cut out-

piano

xylophone

tambourine

# My Tot School Schedule

| Activity | Activity Classification | Date Introduced | Tally of Times Done | Date of Mastery |
|---|---|---|---|---|
| Bombs Away | Fine Motor | August xx, 2014 | 111 | |
| What's that Sound? | Auditory | | | |
| Walk the Box | Gross Motor | | | |
| Tearing Paper | Fine Motor | August xx, 2014 | | |
| | | | | |
| | | | | |
| | | | | |

# My Tot School Schedule

| Activity | Activity Classification | Date Introduced | Tally of Times Done | Date of Mastery |
|---|---|---|---|---|
|  |  |  |  |  |
|  |  |  |  |  |
|  |  |  |  |  |
|  |  |  |  |  |
|  |  |  |  |  |
|  |  |  |  |  |
|  |  |  |  |  |

www.learning2walk.com

Made in the USA
Coppell, TX
18 September 2020